*Philosophical Passages:*
*Wittgenstein, Emerson, Austin, Derrida*

THE BUCKNELL LECTURES IN LITERARY THEORY
*General Editors: Michael Payne and Harold Schweizer*

The lectures in this series explore some of the fundamental changes in literary studies that have occurred during the past thirty years in response to new work in feminism, Marxism, psychoanalysis, and deconstruction. They assess the impact of these changes and examine specific texts in the light of this new work. Each volume in the series includes a critical assessment of the lecturer's own publications, an interview, and a comprehensive bibliography.

# Philosophical Passages:

## Wittgenstein, Emerson, Austin, Derrida

## Stanley Cavell

BLACKWELL
Oxford UK & Cambridge USA

Copyright © Stanley Cavell 1995

The right of Stanley Cavell to be identified as author of this work has been
asserted in accordance with the Copyright, Designs and Patents Act 1988.

First published 1995
Reprinted 1995, 1996

Blackwell Publishers Inc.
238 Main Street
Cambridge, Massachusetts 02142
USA

Blackwell Publishers Ltd
108 Cowley Road
Oxford OX4 1JF
UK

*Library of Congress Cataloging-in-Publication Data*
Cavell, Stanley, 1926–
      Philosophical passages: Wittgenstein, Emerson, Austin, Derrida/
Stanley Cavell.
      p.    cm.–(The Bucknell lectures in literary theory; 12)
      "Stanley Cavell: a working bibliography, 1951–1994/compiled by
Peter S. Fosl": p.
      Includes index.
      ISBN 0–631–19269–7. – ISBN 0–631–19271–9 (pbk.)
      1. Philosophy.    2. Wittgenstein, Ludwig, 1889–1957.    3. Emerson,
Ralph Waldo, 1803–1882 – Philosophy.    4. Austin, J. L. (John Langshaw),
1911–1960.    5. Derrida, Jacques.    6. Philosophy, American – 19th
century.    7. Philosophy, Modern – 20th century.    8. Literature –
Philosophy.    9. Criticism.    I. Title.    II. Series.
B945.C273P48    1995
100–dc20                                                                  94–15838
                                                                                CIP

*British Library Cataloguing in Publication Data*

A CIP catalogue record for this book is available from the British Library.

Typeset in 11 on 13pt Plantin by Best-set Typesetter Ltd, Hong Kong.
Printed in Great Britain by Hartnolls Limited, Bodmin, Cornwall

This book is printed on acid-free paper

# Contents

vi   Contents

# Preface

Fundamental and far-reaching changes in literary studies, often compared to paradigmatic shifts in the sciences, have been taking place during the last thirty years. These changes have included enlarging the literary canon not only to include novels, poems, and plays by writers whose race, gender, or nationality had marginalized their work, but also to include texts by philosophers, psychoanalysts, historians, anthropologists, and social and religious thinkers, who previously were studied by critics merely as "background." The stance of the critic and student of literature is also now more in question than ever before. In 1951 it was possible for Cleanth Brooks to declare with confidence that the critic's job was to describe and evaluate literary objects, implying the relevance for criticism of the model of scientific objectivity, while leaving unasked questions concerning significant issues in scientific theory, such as complementarity, indeterminacy, and the use of metaphor. Now the possibility of value-free skepticism is itself in doubt as many feminist, Marxist, and psychoanalytic theorists have stressed the inescapability of ideology and the consequent obligation of teachers and students of literature to declare their political, axiological, and aesthetic positions in order to make those positions conscious and available for examination. Such expansion and deepening of literary studies has, for many critics, revitalized their field.

Those for whom the theoretical revolution has been regenerative would readily echo, and apply to criticism, Lacan's call to revitalize psychoanalysis: "I consider it to be an urgent task to disengage from concepts that are being deadened by routine use the meaning that they regain both from a re-examination of their history and from a reflexion on their subjective foundations. That, no doubt, is the teacher's prime function."

Many practicing writers and teachers of literature, however, see recent developments in literary theory as dangerous and anti-humanistic. They would insist that displacement of the centrality of the word, claims for the "death of the author," emphasis upon gaps and incapacities in language, and indiscriminate opening of the canon threaten to marginalize literature itself. On this view the advance of theory is possible only because of literature's retreat in the face of aggressive moves by Marxism, feminism, deconstruction, and psychoanalysis. Furthermore, at a time of militant conservatism and the dominance of corporate values in America and Western Europe, literary theory threatens to diminish further the declining audience for literature and criticism. Theoretical books are difficult to read; they usually assume that their readers possess knowledge that few who have received a traditional literary education have; they often require massive reassessments of language, meaning, and the world; they seem to draw their life from suspect branches of other disciplines: professional philosophers usually avoid Derrida; psychoanalysts dismiss Freud as unscientific; Lacan was excommunicated even by the International Psycho-Analytical Association.

The volumes in this series record part of the attempt at Bucknell University to sustain conversation about changes in literary studies, the impact of those changes on literary art, and the significance of literary theory for the humanities and human sciences. A generous grant from the Andrew W. Mellon Foundation has made possible a five-year series of visiting lectureships by internationally known participants in the reshaping of literary studies. Each volume includes a comprehensive introduction to the published work of the lecturer, the Bucknell Lectures, an interview, and a comprehensive bibliography.

# Acknowledgments

The editors wish to thank the many students and faculty who participated in the Mellon Seminars in Literary Theory at Bucknell, especially during the spring of 1993, when Stanley Cavell delivered the lectures included in this volume. Brian Truglio, Tara Gilligan, and Kristine Dane helped with the first stages of this book. Theresa Wenzke provided invaluable assistance in the updating of Peter Fosl's bibliography, an earlier version of which appeared in "The Senses of Stanley Cavell," eds Richard Fleming and Michael Payne (*Bucknell Review*, 32:1, 1989). We are also pleased to acknowledge the support of the Andrew W. Mellon Foundation, Frances Fergusson, and Andrew McNeillie of Blackwell Publishers, which made this series possible.

We are grateful to Oxford University Press, Inc., New York, for permission to quote from *The Claim of Reason* by Stanley Cavell (© Oxford University Press, Inc., 1979).

# Introduction

## Cavell's Voices and Derrida's Grammatology

The stature of Stanley Cavell is increasingly considered unique among living American philosophers because of the range and power of his thought, the depth of his influence on a newly emerging generation of thinkers, and the potential of his work to provide a means of exchange among Anglo-American and Continental European philosophers.[1] Cavell's writings on Shakespeare have contributed to the criticism of the tragedies the most sustained philosophical meditation on the scope and limits of Shakespeare's skepticism since Schopenhauer and Nietzsche; his two books on film have brought philosophical imagination and discipline to the study of popular motion pictures, while providing aesthetics with exemplary objects for discussion that are as close to common coin as anything in modern American culture; his study of Thoreau's *Walden* and the essays of Emerson have recovered a tradition of American philosophy that was in danger of being repressed, lost, or purposefully broken; and his writings on Wittgenstein, Austin, and the traditions of philosophy from Plato, Descartes, and Locke through Kant, Nietzsche, and Heidegger have both made possible a reclamation of those traditions for contemporary philosophy and introduced into Cavell's own writing the powerful resonance of other voices to counter or accompany his own, which is itself strikingly original but at the same time deeply traditional.

Although the essays in *Must We Mean What We Say?* (1969) or in *Themes Out of School* (1984) may provide a gentler introduction to Cavell's thought, the opening paragraphs to Part One of *The Claim of Reason* (1979) are perhaps the best place to begin reading him. These now famous (or infamous) pages are ostensibly directions for reading Wittgenstein's *Philosophical Investigations*, a text to which Cavell has often returned. There Cavell advises that *Philosophical Investigations* should be considered as a text rather than as a set of problems; that its quality may be inferred from the quality of other texts it arouses or stimulates others to write; that it is essentially a written text, however much Wittgenstein's human voice may be heard in it; that it is not simply a text which can be "approached" as though it stood forever at some distance from the reader; that its language not only invokes ordinary notions and experience but also discrepancies from the ordinary; that Wittgenstein's immediate audience – grounded in the empiricist tradition of philosophy – includes precisely those who will be most intimately offended by his text; that he appeals to his readers to form a community around his text, the search for such a community being also the search for reason.

In the process of offering these observations on reading Wittgenstein, Cavell also implies that he is proposing a set of protocols for reading all philosophical texts. It is surely not coincidental, therefore, that these comments should serve as a useful guide to reading Cavell himself. Both Wittgenstein's and Cavell's works are textually self-conscious; and their own words, whether from an earlier part of their text or from an earlier work, are often brought forward by quotation or citation in order (like a compressed spring) to provide the forward thrust of their present thought. Cavell's practice elaborates on

Wittgenstein's creation of a philosophical style that oper-
ates simultaneously on two levels. One is the level of an
imitation of the human voice. Although many writers do
not speak at all in the manner in which they write, one of
the great appeals of Cavell's writing – what is often called
its "charm" by those who have heard him in lecture or in
conversation – is the continuity of his spoken and written
voices. (The seminar and interview in this volume provide
a vivid sense of this continuity.) Although it may be tempting to assume, therefore, a "naturalness" or "ordinariness"
in Cavell's written style, his writer's art is powerfully at
work in the creation of a fiction of speech out of the
medium of written language. Similarly, his spoken language is often classically oratorical. Drawing thus simultaneously on the arts of spoken and written language,
Cavell's style (like Lacan's) also recalls the earliest medium of philosophy: the Platonic dialogue, which in part is
a fiction of spoken conversation.

But more explicitly, on this first level of his style,
Cavell's rhetorical art invokes, elaborates, and combats the
oracular conventions of Emerson. Cavell first wrote of his
long struggle with Emerson in the two essays appended to
*The Senses of Walden* in 1981, but he has written more
persistently and openly about Emerson as a philosopher in
*This New Yet Unapproachable America: Lectures after
Emerson after Wittgenstein* (1989) and *Conditions Handsome
and Unhandsome: The Constitution of Emersonian Perfectionism* (1990). Emerson's legacy has recently been much
contested by such writers as Harold Bloom, William Gass,
Irving Howe, and Richard Poirier. No small part of recent
re-readings of Emerson has been the sense that, despite
the argument of "The American Scholar," he was a trans-
atlantic philosopher, profoundly responsive to European
thinkers, some of whom – Nietzsche especially and perhaps surprisingly – responded enthusiastically to his
work.[2] For Emerson (and, it would seem, for Cavell) "the
right state" of man is "Man Thinking," not man as "a mere

thinker, or still worse, the parrot of other men's thinking."
When Man Thinking becomes a reader, the book he reads
is "luminous with manifold allusion. Every sentence is
doubly significant, and the sense of our author is as broad
as the world" ("The American Scholar"). The thought in
the texts he reads is a manifestation of "the intellect con-
structive," which has the power to make the thought acces-
sible and available for participation by means of "a vehicle
or art by which it is conveyed to men. To be communicable
it must become picture or sensible object" ("Intellect").
The creation of such pictures or sensible objects "does not
come by study, but by the intellect being where and what
it sees; by sharing the path or circuit of things through
forms, and so making them translucid to others" ("The
Poet"). The philosopher, finally, "is more than an expert,
or a schoolman, or a geometer, or the prophet of a peculiar
message. He represents the privilege of the intellect, the
power namely, of carrying up every fact to successive
platforms and so disclosing in every fact a germ of expansion. These expansions are in the essence of thought"
("Plato; or the Philosopher").[3]

In addition to the articulate voice of Man Thinking in
Cavell's style – its open invitation to participative reading,
its creation of vivid images that convey the thought, and its
exfoliating expansiveness – Cavell's style, on a second
level, makes precise demands and sets exact terms for his
reader's participation. Before introducing himself in *The
Claim of Reason*, thus reserving the first-person pronoun
for his second paragraph, Cavell insists that his reader
enter the text through a labyrinthine first sentence of two
hundred and sixteen words. Man Thinking is, on this
second level of style, Cavell Thinking: his is another
unique voice, distinct from Emerson's and Wittgenstein's.
Although Cavell beckons his reader to an intimate engagement with his thought, he also seeks to provoke by the
demanding terms on which he invites engagement. But
from these textual demands, a fragile community of plea-

sure and agon develops. For Cavell, however, the doubt lingers that the community may be as yet a "claim to community": "I have nothing more to go on than my conviction, my sense that I make sense. It may prove to be the case that I am wrong, that my conviction isolates me, from all others, from myself." Emerson shared this same uncertainty.

In the pages that follow Cavell provides extraordinarily careful and sustained readings of Emerson's "Fate"; Derrida's response to J. L. Austin in "Signature Event Context"; and Wittgenstein's *Philosophical Investigations*. These lectures make available some of Cavell's most recent thinking on these texts, while also looking back on his efforts to reappropriate Emerson as a philosophical writer, to demonstrate the subtle power of Austin's thought, and to hear the voice of philosophy in *Philosophical Investigations*. The reading of "Fate" continues Cavell's investigation of Emerson's concept of thinking, which he began in the first chapter of *Conditions Handsome and Unhandsome*. The reply to Derrida's remarks on Austin not only places Austin's theory of performative utterances in the context of his other writing but also recalls Austin's importance as a teacher and as an early influence on Cavell. (This text also anticipates a portion of the forthcoming Jerusalem Lectures, entitled *A Pitch of Philosophy*.) "Notes and Afterthoughts on the Opening of Wittgenstein's *Investigations*" provides the rare opportunity of witnessing Cavell in the act of teaching a philosophical text. These much revised and updated notes, which have been circulating in manuscript since 1991 but are published here for the first time, were the basis of a portion of Cavell's lecture courses on the *Investigations*, which he gave at Berkeley and later at Harvard. They in part look back on the opening pages of *The Claim of Reason*.

Cavell's "What Did Derrida Want of Austin?," his response to Derrida's "Signature Event Context," perhaps requires a brief explanation. Derrida's paper was originally delivered at a conference on communication in Montreal in 1971, which was sponsored by the International Congress of Societies of French Language Philosophy. Its publication in English in 1977 sparked a reply form John Searle, whose *Speech Acts*, as Cavell observes, has become better known than Austin's writings on which it is based. Derrida responded to Searle in turn, producing a series of exchanges that culminated in the publication of Derrida's *Limited Inc.* (1988). What began as a serious philosophical debate – in part over a reading of Austin – finally spilled over into a running scandal in the pages of *The New York Review of Books* and in an attempt by the president of the American Philosophical Association to convince the French government to veto the unanimous election of Derrida as Director of the International College of Philosophy on the charge of *obscurantisme terroriste*.[4]

"Signature Event Context" is divided into four sections. Part One asks the provocative question, given the occasion of the conference, Is the word "*communication*" communicable? That is, is that word able to correspond to and to transmit a concept that is unique, univocal, and controllable? To ask this question at all would seem to require an anticipation of the meaning of the word and in turn a large set of assumptions about language. Those assumptions might be gathered together this way: What I want is to know what I think, to have the words to express my thoughts clearly in such a way as to have my idea received by another, understood, and mutually affirmed as true. Communication, then would be in Derrida's words "a means of transport or transitional medium . . . of a unified meaning." This definition, however, impoverishes the word by depriving it of its polysemous and non-semantic signification, which includes the displacement of "force". It is not that *communication* has a literal or primary meaning, plus other (for example, metaphorical) meanings. Presumably that would assume that we already know that metaphor is somehow secondary or not linguistically normal. Perhaps, then, *communication* can be stabilized or "reduced" by referring to "context": but are the conditions of a context absolutely determinable? Derrida says they are not. Furthermore, if they are not determinable, the current concept of context is inadequate; and the current concept of writing as a form of communication must be reassessed. Such a reassessment is the project of Derrida's grammatology.[5]

Part Two of Derrida's text takes up the current concept of writing as having the potential to extend the power and range of communication beyond speech and gesture. The assumption here is that the unity of meaning can be transmitted through a homogeneous field. Furthermore, this conception of writing has long been proper to philosophy. However curious, the locus classicus of this view is Condillac's appropriation of Warburton's *Divine Legation of Moses*, which Derrida summarizes this way:

> If men write it is (1) because they have to communicate; (2) because what they have to communicate is their "thought," their "ideas," their representations. Thought, as representation, precedes and governs communication, which transports the "idea," the signified content; (3) because men are *already* in a state that allows them to communicate their thought to themselves and to each other when, in a continuous manner, they invent the particular means of communication, writing.[6]

The implication of this formula, Derrida observes, is that writing is simply a passive medium of thought, that it will have no effect on meaning.

Given this view of writing as representation that makes the thought present in another place, the examples of Egyptian hieroglyphic and Chinese ideographic writing are emblematic of the pictorial aspiration of all writing. Thus, in Condillac's view, the history of writing proceeds from painting to the letter. But in his chapter on writing in "On the Origins and Progress of Language," Condillac emphasizes the point that writing makes thought "known to persons who are absent." Representation supplants (supplements) presence, which Condillac sees as continuous and without a break. In this respect Condillac transmits an ideology of representation.

Having invoked or appropriated Condillac's argument, Derrida proceeds to elaborate on it by expanding its implications. Every sign – including gestures, articulated language, and writing – presupposes a certain absence. But what is written remains readable even in the absence of the receiver, as for example, if a letter is deferred, intercepted, or not delivered. But to claim that writing is repeatable or iterable ties writing to the other, ties repetition to alterity. Similarly, for writing to be writing, it must function without presence – that is, in the absence of the sender – although his signature would seem (poignantly or pathetically) to convey his desire to say what he means.

What then are the nuclear traits of writing? It breaks with the conception of communication as the transmission of consciousness or presence. It disengages from the semantic or hermeneutic horizon of meaning, in the sense of intentional or prescribed (that is, pre-written) meaning. It is a form of dissemination that disqualifies the limiting concept inscription, and it carries with it a force that breaks with its context or presence at the moment of its inscription. Furthermore, these features of writing, Derrida insists, are also features of all language and all experience.

In Part Three Derrida turns to Austin, apparently for two reasons: first, because Austin's account of performative utterances already called into question the idea of communication formulated by Condillac; but also because the critique Austin begins, Derrida thinks, is not taken far enough.[7] Indeed, the phrase from Austin that Derrida uses as a headnote to his paper – "Still confining ourselves for simplicity to *spoken* utterance" – anticipates his criticism of Austin's artificially limited view of language. There is much, however, that Derrida affirms in Austin. Although

Austin considers speech acts as communication, his distinction between *constantive utterances* (true or false descriptions of facts) and *performative utterances* (utterances that accomplish something through speech itself) opens up the category of communication to what is other than the transmission of thought-content. Performative utterances do not have "outside" referents; they rather transmit force, as Nietzsche seemed to anticipate. Austin's achievement then, in Derrida's view, was to shatter the classical concept of communication, but he limited his argument too soon. For performative utterances to be felicitous, they must occur within certain contextual conventions. But Derrida points out that there are also intrinsic conventions to language; that the possiblility of infelicity is inescapable; that what Austin calls parasitic in language excludes more than citation, which actually may be the *sine qua non* of performatives; that Austin excludes drama, poetry, and writing. In order to fend off infelicity and parasitical utterances, Austin invokes present, conscious intention as a defining context. To this, Derrida opposes his concept of *différance* the irreducible absence of intention which is inescapable in all language, even in the word *communication*. Derrida concludes that Austin requires the source of the utterance as a continuing presence, or at least as secured by a signature. But signatures are susceptible (as Derrida argues in Part Four) to the problems of all language: absence, iterability, detachedness from their event, and independence of context. Like all forms and structures, they invite deconstruction, or perform it in advance of being detected. Thus, they reverse classical oppositions and displace accustomed conceptual orders.

Derrida's reading of Austin and Cavell's reading of that reading invite the speculation that there may be genres of philosophy, as there are of drama. When Hegel proposes his theory of negativity – the incorporated, previously designated limit of the spirit that has since been breached – is his affirmation of what has been violated an embracing of tragedy, or is his transcendent appropriation of breached limit and the concept of death an affirmation of comic inclusiveness? When Descartes finds it possible to affirm an infinite capacity that makes possible a finite mind's sense of the infinite, is this – after all the careful doubt that has gone before – a turn toward a divinely comic inclusiveness, or is his relentless, isolated doubt fundamentally tragic? Similar questions are left to readers of Cavell and Derrida, each of whom writes passionately and provocatively on the forms and persistence of philosophy and on the inescapability of skepticism, tragedy, and mortality. The one, perhaps a spokesman, the other perhaps an inscriber. In which medium did philosophy begin, and in which does it continue? That strange drawing by Matthew Paris of Socrates writing in response to Plato's apparent dictation only helps to epitomize this perennial question. While Derrida reads the writing of philosophy, Cavell listens to its voice.

**Michael Payne**

NOTES

1   See the studies of Cavell in the bibliography at the end of this book. In this introduction I have borrowed and rewritten some sentences from my introduction to *The Senses of Stanley Cavell*, eds Richard Fleming and Michael Payne (Lewisburg: Bucknell University Press, 1989), pp. 13–18. I am grateful to the editor and publishers of *Bucknell Review* for permission to reproduce these sentences and to include those portions of Peter Wasel [now Fosl]'s bibliography that appeared in an earlier version in *The Senses of Stanley Cavell*, pp. 322–34.

2   For a preliminary survey of these responses, see my "Emerson, Nietzsche, and the Politics of Interpretation," *CEA Forum*, 18 (1988), pp.16–18.

3 Citations from Emerson are from *Essays and Lectures*, ed. Joel Porte (New York: Library of America, 1983).

4 Jacques Derrida, *Limited Inc.*, ed. Gerald Graff (Evanston, IL: Northwestern University Press, 1988), pp. 158–9.

5 It is perhaps obvious that in this attempt to provide a context for Cavell's response to Derrida, I am bracketing the cautions about context that Derrida specifies. For further discussion of Cavell and Derrida, see Michael Fischer, *Stanley Cavell and Literary Skepticism* (Chicago: The University of Chicago Press, 1989), esp. p. 61.

6 Derrida, p. 4. Derrida has written at greater length about Condillac in *The Archeology of the Frivolous: Reading Condillac*, trans. John P. Leavey, Jr. (Lincoln: University of Nebraska Press, 1973) and *Of Grammatology*, trans, G. C. Spivak (Baltimore: The Johns Hopkins University Press, 1976), Part Two, ch. 4.

7 Derrida often finds a positive ground for his critiques of other writers in their incomplete critiques of predecessors, such as Condillac's of Warburton, Heidegger's of Nietzsche, or Lévi-Strauss's of Rousseau.

# Emerson's Constitutional Amending: Reading "Fate"

What follows is the latest installment of a project, or experiment, of about a dozen years' standing, to re-appropriate Emerson (I sometimes call this overcoming his repression) as a philosophical writer. I am aware of a number of reasons for my interest in such a project. Since Emerson is characteristically said – by his admirers as well as by his detractors – not to be a philosopher (no one known to me in the history of Western thought is so obsessively denied the title of philosopher), my thought was that if I could understand this denial I would learn something not only about Emerson, and not only about American culture, but something about philosophy, about what makes it painful.

If the thought of Emerson's work as constituting philosophy – or, as I sometimes put it, as calling for philosophy – is considered, then something further could be considered. It is more or less obvious, and is given more or less significance by various philosophers, that Western philosophy has, roughly since the death of Kant, been split between two traditions, call them the German and the English traditions; and each of these has its internal splits. I take Wittgenstein as the culmination of one line of English-speaking philosophy arising from the work of Frege and Russell; and I take Heidegger as the culmination of one line of German-speaking philosophy arising from the work of Hegel and Husserl. I am not alone in regarding Wittgenstein and Heidegger as perhaps the two major voices of philosophy in the middle third of this century. Yet it seems to me that no one – however intelligent or culti- vated – is equally at home, say equally creative, with the writing of both; so that the distance between them, in content and in procedure, remains to my mind unmea- sured. I might say that to inherit philosophy now means to me to inherit it as split.

Against this rough background, the figure of Emerson represents for me (along with Thoreau) a mode of thinking and writing I feel I am in a position to avail myself of, a mode which at the same time can be seen to underlie the thinking of both Wittgenstein and of Heidegger – so that Emerson may become a site from which to measure the difficulties within each and between both.

The lecture to follow is a continuation of the work of the first chapter of my recently published *Conditions Handsome and Unhandsome*, concerning Emerson's concept of think- ing, a concept I call aversive thinking. That title alludes to a sentence of Emerson's from "Self-Reliance": "Self-reli- ance is [the] aversion [of conformity]." Emerson finds that conformity is the virtue in most request – by which he means it is the primary force of our social existence. By "self-reliance" I take him, correspondingly, to mean the essay of that title, and by synecdoche, his individual body of writing. So for him to say "self-reliance is the aversion of conformity" is to say that his writing and his society inces- santly recoil from, or turn away from one another; but since this is incessant, the picture is at the same time of each incessantly turning *toward* the other. But why call this writing *thinking*?

Emerson characterizes thinking as marked by transfigu- ration and by conversion. I will merely assert here that these predicates refer essentially to the action of words, under subjection to some kind of figuration, in causing understanding or illumination on a par with that of religion – the religion always under criticism (held in aversion) – in Emerson's thought. My claim is accordingly that the sentence "Self-Reliance is the aversion of conformity," when itself subjected to the operation of transfiguration and conversion, means something like: To think is to turn around, or to turn back (Wittgenstein says lead back), the words of ordinary life (hence the present forms of our lives) that now repel thought, disgust it. (Repels him, Emerson, of course, but he is also part of that life, which is therefore disgusted with itself.)

The only way to become convinced of such a reading, and its possible significance, is of course to try it out in scores of instances. We will see some cases in what follows from the essay "Fate."

Before beginning on that, I should say why it is just now in my adventure with Emerson that I choose, or feel forced, for the first time to emphasize a political theme in his work. I specify a brief answer at the close of these remarks, but I might indicate at once the general stakes in play. I have over the years ever more closely linked Emerson and Heidegger through the intermediary of Nietzsche, who is intimately, pervasively involved in the thinking of each. In *Conditions Handsome and Unhandsome* I associate each of them in a view of the moral life I call Emersonian Perfectionism – at a moment in which the revelations of Heidegger's lasting investments in Nazism were producing a new convulsion of response from at least half of the Western philosophical world. Does Heidegger's politics – by association, to say the least – taint Emerson's points of contact with it?

The essay "Fate" is perhaps Emerson's principal statement about the human condition of freedom, even about something Emerson calls the paradox that freedom is necessary; we might formulate this as the human fatedness to freedom. This comes to speaking of the human fatedness to thinking, since "Intellect annuls Fate. So far as a man thinks, he is free. . . . The revelation of Thought takes man out of servitude into freedom." Could it be that the founder of American thinking, writing this essay in 1850, just months after the passage of the Fugitive Slave Law, whose support by Daniel Webster we know Emerson to have been unforgettably, unforgivingly horrified by, was in this essay not thinking about the American institution of slavery? I think it cannot be. Then why throughout the distressed, difficult, dense stretches of metaphysical speculation of this essay does Emerson seem mostly, even essentially, to keep silent on the subject of slavery, make nothing special of it? It is a silence that must still encourage his critics, as not long ago his admirer Harold Bloom and his detractor John Updike, to imagine that Emerson gave up on the hope of democracy. But since I am continuing to follow out the consequences of finding in Emerson the founding of American thinking – the consequence, for example, that his thought is repressed in the culture he founded – the irony of discovering that this repressed thinking has given up on the hope and demand for a nation of the self-governing, would be, so I fear, harder than I could digest.

I was myself silent about this question of Emerson's silence when I wrote an essay in 1983 mostly on Emerson's "Fate" (I called it "Emerson, Coleridge, Kant"), my first somewhat extended treatment of an Emersonian text. It was seeming to me so urgent then to see to the claim of Emerson as a philosophical writer, in principle imaginable as founding philosophy for a nation still finding itself, that I suppose I recurrently hoped that Emerson had, for the moment of the essay "Fate," sufficiently excused or justified his silence in saying there, "Nothing is more disgusting than the crowing about liberty by slaves, as most men are." But no sooner would I see this as an excuse or justification for silence than it would seem empty to me, so that I could never appeal to it. Isn't the statement that most men are slaves merely a weak, metaphorical way of feeling and of speaking, one that blunts both the fact of literal slavery and the facts of the particular ways in which we freely sell ourselves out? How is this conventional use of words essentially different from the sort of "[shameful capitulation] to badges and names, to large societies and dead institutions" that had so chagrined Emerson in "Self-Reliance":

> If malice and vanity wear the coat of philanthropy, shall that pass? If an angry bigot assumes this bountiful cause of Abolition, and comes to me with his last news from Barbados, why should I not say to him, 'Go love thy infant; love thy woodchopper; be good-natured and modest; have that grace; and never varnish your hard, uncharitable ambition with this incredible tenderness for black folk a thousand miles off. Thy love afar is spite at home.'

It is not news that high philosophy can be used to cover low practice; nor that the love in philanthropy is tainted. Is Emerson so in doubt about the state of his own malice and vanity and anger and bigotry and charity and love that he has to clear them up before he can say clearly that he sides against slavery?

On March 7, 1854, Emerson delivered a lecture called "The Fugitive Slave Law," marking the fourth anniversary of Webster's decisive speech in favor of that legislation. Emerson's lecture goes this way:

> Nobody doubts that Daniel Webster could make a good speech. Nobody doubts that there were good and plausible things to be said on the part of the South. But this is not a question of ingenuity, not a question of syllogisms, but of sides. *How came he there?* . . . There are always texts and thoughts and arguments. . . . There was the same law in England for Jeffries and Talbot and Yorke to read slavery out of, and for Lord Mansfield to read freedom. . . . But the question which History will ask [of Webster] is broader. In the final hour when he was forced by the peremptory necessity of the closing armies to take a side, – did he take the part of great principles, the side of human-

ity and justice, or the side of abuse and oppression and
chaos? (*Emerson's Works*, XI, *Miscellanies*, ed. J. E. Cabot,
1883)

So Emerson names and would avoid, both those at home
who choose to interpret the law so as to take the side
on behalf of slavery near, as well as those who in "Self-
Reliance" he had named angry bigots incredibly varnish-
ing their uncharitable ambition at home by taking the
side against slavery afar. Both may count as what Emerson
describes as "crowing about liberty by slaves"; and
his refusal of crowing (for or against) would perhaps be
what strikes one as his essential silence on the subject
precisely in an essay on freedom paradoxically entitled
"Fate."

The suggestion is that there is a way of taking sides that
is not crowing, a different way of having a say in this
founding matter of slavery. If Emerson is who I think he is,
then how he finds his way to having his say, how he
undertakes to think – whether, most particularly, he is
serious (as opposed to what? – literary?) in his claim that
"so far as a man thinks, he is free" – is as fateful for
America's claim to its own culture of thinking as its success in ridding itself of the institution of slavery will be for
establishing its claim to have discovered a new world,
hence to exist.

We have to ask what kind of writing – philosophical?
political? religious? – takes the form of the pent, prophetic
prose of "Fate." Emerson speaks there also (as well as later
in "Fugitive Slave Law") of the taking of a side. His
formulation in "Fate" is of the capacity, when a person
finds himself a victim of his fate – for example, "ground to
powder by the vice of his race" – to "take sides with the
Deity who secures universal benefit by his pain." This may
strike one as the formulation less of a course of action than
of inaction. But take Emerson's reference in his phrase
"the vice of his race" (by which a person finds himself
victimized) to be specified in the description earlier in the

essay of "expensive races – race living at the expense of race." But *which* vice does "expensive" suggest? The literal context of that predicate takes the races in question as the human race living at the expense of the races of animals that serve us as food: "You have just dined, and however scrupulously the slaughter-house is concealed in the graceful distance of miles, there is complicity, expensive races." It happens that we can produce evidence that this passage about human carnivorousness, and its companion human gracefulness in keeping its conditions concealed from itself, is a parable about the cannibalism, as it were, in living gracefully off other *human* races. The evidence comes from an early paragraph in Emerson's address "On Emancipation in the British West Indies," delivered in 1844, the tenth anniversary of that emancipation legislation, the year of Emerson's breakthrough essay "Experience." In Emerson's West Indies address, he remarks that "From the earliest monuments it appears that one race was victim and served the other races," and that "the negro has been an article of luxury to the commercial nations"; and he goes on to say there, "Language must be raked, the secrets of the slaughter-houses and infamous holes that cannot front the day, must be ransacked, to tell what negro-slavery has been". (Cabot edition, XI, 133, 134)

I propose to take "Fate" pervasively – beyond the reach of the sort of textual intersection I just adduced as evidence – as something I might call a philosophical enactment of freedom, a parable of the struggle against slavery not as a general metaphor for claiming human freedom, but as the absolute image of the necessary siding against fate toward freedom that is the condition of philosophical thinking; as if the aspiration to freedom is philosophy's breath.

Doesn't the sheer eloquence of the West Indies address compromise this proposal from the outset? – with its demand to rake language and ransack slaughter-houses to tell of negro slavery. And again, always again, the question returns whether Emerson in "Fate" – the same man who younger, in that earlier West Indies address, confessed himself heart-sick to read the history of that slavery – isn't courting the danger of seeming to avoid the sickening facts of the slavery that continues not metaphysically afar but at home?

What is he thinking of – whom is he thinking of – when in "Fate" he says, "In the history of the individual there is an account of his condition, and he knows himself to be party to his present estate"? If the sentences of "Fate" are to be brought to the condition of slavery, are we to imagine this statement about the individual knowing himself to be party to his estate to be said to the individual who is in the condition of enslavement? What would prevent this announcement from constituting the obscene act of blaming the slave for his slavery? (My intermittent sense of this possibility, and of the fact that I had no satisfying answer to it, was brought home to me by a letter from Professor Barbara Packer, whose book *Emerson's Fall* is indispensable to readers of Emerson, following a brief conversation between us concerning Emerson's politics. She writes in her letter of her sense of what I called obscene announcement in "Fate" as something that she had yet to bring under control, and asked for my thoughts. That was in the autumn of 1989. The present version of this essay, meant to collect and incorporate those thoughts, was composed the following year.)

An implication of saying "you know yourself party to your estate" – if it is not pure blame – is that you are free to leave it. John Brown might say something of the sort, without obscenity, to a person in the condition of enslavement, given that he would be saying, if with a certain derangement, "I know the only way to exercise your freedom to leave your estate is to court death, and I'll court it with you." And Walt Whitman might say something related, as in the altogether remarkable "I Sing the Body Electric," in which he watches the man's body at auction and the woman's body at auction, and he declares his love for, his sameness with, the body – hence, he declares, with the soul – of the slave. What gives to the knowledge of American slavery the absoluteness of its pain is the knowledge that these human beings in that condition, in persisting to live, persist in taking part in every breath in interpreting and preserving what a human existence can bear. But do we imagine that Emerson, like John Brown and Walt Whitman, has a way to bear the knowledge of that pain – he who is habitually supposed to have turned aside from the philosophically tragic sense of life?

Then perhaps Emerson only means to say of us Northerners, neither slaves nor slave owners, that we are party to our estate – meaning perhaps that we make ourselves slaves to, let us say, the interests of Southern slave owners that never even paid for us. But that is not exactly news. Emerson reports in the West Indies address that when "three hundred thousand persons in Britain pledged themselves to abstain from all articles of island produce . . . the planters were obliged to give way . . . and the slave trade was abolished." Such responses to slavery as economic boycott are evidently not Emerson's business in "Fate." Whom, then, in that mood, is he writing to? Who are we who read him then?

If "taking sides with the Deity" does not, for Emerson, (just) mean taking the right side in the crowing about slavery, the side Daniel Webster failed to take as the armies were closing on the issue, how might it be taken? Here is more context from "Fate": "A man must ride alternately on the horses of his private and his public nature. . . . Leaving the daemon who suffers, he is to take sides with the Deity who secures universal benefit by his pain." That the human being is the being who *can* take a representative – public – stance, knows the (moral, objective) imperative to the stance, is familiar and recurrent Emersonian – not to say Kantian – ground; nothing is a more founding fact for him. I read this Platonic image here about riding alternately the horses of human nature, so that taking sides with the Deity is a refusal to take sides in the human *crowing* over slavery. Emerson's turn to take sides with the Deity, like and unlike the political extremity of Locke's appeal to Heaven is not exactly a call to revolution but a claim to prophecy. (*Second Treatise*, chapter XIV, section 168, chapter XIX, section 242.) "Leaving the daemon who suffers" means leaving one's private, limited passions on the subject of slavery, for or against.

What is the alternative horse, the public expression of a beneficial pain (given in the absence of a constituted public, since so much of the human voice, the slave's voice, is unrepresented in that public)? The alternative is, let us say, not venting your pain, but maintaining it; in the present case, writing every sentence in pain. (Freud comparably says: remembering rather than repeating something.) It contains the pain of refusing human sides, shunning argument, with every breath. The time of argument is over. Where is pain's benefit? Is philosophy over?

At the opening of "Fate," Emerson says "We are incompetent to solve the times. . . . To me . . . the question of the times resolved itself into a practical question of the conduct of life." I have in effect said that in "Fate" the "question of the times" – what Emerson calls in his opening "the huge orbits of the prevailing ideas" whose return and opposition we cannot "reconcile," and what he describes near his close by saying, "Certain ideas are in the air" – is the question of slavery; and certain ideas in the air, accordingly, are emancipation and secession, issues producing the compromise of 1850, which concerned – besides the Fugitive Slave Act – the slave trade, and the admission of territories into the union with or without slaves. Setting out the terms for "the greatest debate in Congressional history" (*Documents of American History*, ed. Henry Steele Commager, New York, 1958, p. 319), Henry Clay prefaces his Resolutions of compromise by saying, "It being desirable, for the peace, concord and harmony of the Union of these States to settle and adjust amicably all existing questions of controversy between them, arising out of the institution of slavery, upon a fair, equitable and just basis; therefore," – and then follows eight paragraphs each beginning with the word "Resolved" or the words "But, resolved." Emerson in effect prefaces "Fate" by speaking, in his opening paragraph, as noted, of our incompetence to *solve* the times, and of *resolving* the question of the times; in the second paragraph he states that "The riddle of the age has for each a private *solution*"; and continuing in effect to reverse or recapture the word "Resolved" Emerson says in the middle of "Fate," "Thought *dissolves* the material universe by carrying the mind up into a sphere where all is plastic"; and in the closing paragraphs he speaks of a "solution to the mysteries of human condition" and of "the Blessed Unity which holds nature and soul in perfect solution." This is not Henry Clay's imagined union.

Of course Emerson is quite aware that compared with Henry Clay, and the Houses of Congress, his words about resolution and unity will sound, at best, or at first, private, not to say ethereal. But he seems somehow also to know that he is speaking with necessity ("Our thought, though it were only an hour old, affirms an oldest necessity"), and speaking with universality (being thrown "on the party and interest of the Universe [i.e., taking sides with the Deity] against all and sundry; against ourselves as much as others"). Now necessity and universality are the marks, according to the Kantian philosophy, of the a priori, that is, of human objectivity; so if Emerson's claim is valid, it is the opposing party who is riding the horse of privacy, of what Emerson also calls selfishness, something he would have taken Henry Clay's use of the word "desirable" to have amounted to.

We of course must ask – since Emerson would also know, as well as what is called the next man, that anyone can *claim* to be speaking on the part and interest of the universe and on the side of the Deity – what the source is of his conviction in his own objectivity, his ability, as he puts it in the poem he composed as an epigraph for "Fate," to read omens traced in the air. I understand the source to be his conviction that his abilities are not exclusive, that he claims to know only what everyone knows.

Toward the close of the essay: "The truth is in the air, and the most impressionable brain will announce it first, but *all* will announce it a few minutes later." Emerson is not even saying that *he* is announcing it first, since the truth that is in the air is also, always already, philosophy; it contains not just the present cries for freedom and union and the arguments against them, but perennial cries and arguments. This is surely something the gesture means that Emerson so habitually enjoys making, of listing his predecessors and benefactors – that they are the benefactors of the race, part of our air, our breath. In the essay "Fate" he cites the names of Napolean, Burke, Webster, Kossuth; Jenny Lind; Homer, Zoroaster, Menu; Fulton, Franklin, Watt; Copernicus, Newton, Laplace; Thales, Anaximenes, Empedocles, Pythagorus; Hafiz, Voltaire, Christopher Wren, Dante, Columbus, Goethe, Hegel, Metternich, Adams, Calhoun, Guizot, Peel, Rothschild, Astor, Herodotus, Plutarch. And he says: "The air is full of men." (Emerson puts those words in quotation marks without saying who or what he is quoting. Bartlett's Quotations contains the line "In the air men shall be seen" in a list of rhymed prophecies attributed to Mother Shipton, according to Bartlett's editors a witch and prophetess fabricated in the seventeenth century. I'll have a suggestion about why Emerson might have wanted in this essay to associate himself with such a figure.)

I associate the men in the air with – as in Emerson's epigraph poem – "Birds with auguries on their wings/[who] Chanted undeceiving things,/Him to beckon, him to warn." The "few minutes later" Emerson calculates between the first announcements of truth and, for example, his own impressionable announcings of it – which the world may measure as millennia but which are a few minutes of eternity – are equally no more than the few minutes between, for example, our reading Emerson's pages (his wings of augury, flapping as we turn them forth and back, before us, above our horizon) and our announcing or pronouncing, if just to ourselves, what is chanted from them (not crowed). I have noted elsewhere another of Emerson's master figures for a page of his writing – that of its representing a "standard," that is, a measure to aspire to, specified concretely as a flag, to which to rally oneself. This idea of a standard – by which "Self-Reliance" alludes at the same time to Kant's idea of humankind's two "standpoints" – takes pages one at a time; whereas "wings" pictures them as paired, bound symmetrically on the two sides of a spine.

As with his great reader Thoreau, Emerson loves playing with time, that is, making time vanish where truth is concerned: " 'Tis only a question of time," he says casually a few minutes later in "Fate" than, and as a kind of answer to, the earlier, more portentous phrasing, "the question of the times." (In invoking the idea of the casual, as one characteristic tone he gives his prose, I am thinking of Emerson's characteristic association of that idea with the idea of causality; as if he misses no opportunity for showing that we do not see our fate because we imagine that it is most extraordinary and not yet; rather than most ordinary, and already, like our words.)

Emerson's philosophical sentence strikes the time of conversion and transfiguration that he calls thinking, the time – past crowing – of aversion (inversion, perversion, subversion, "unsettling all things," verses, reversals, tropes, turns, dancing, chanting . . .).

Here are three successive sentences to this effect from "Fate": First, "If the Universe have these savage accidents, our atoms are savage in resistance." That is, speaking philosophically, or universally, "accidents" are opposed to "necessities," and in thus implying that slavery is accidental, or arbitrary, and resistance to it necessary and natural,

Emerson takes away its chief argument. Second, "We should be crushed by the atmosphere but for the reaction of the air within the body." That is, the ideas that are in the air are our life's breath; they become our words; slavery is supported by some of them and might have crushed the rest of them; uncrushed, they live in opposition. Third, "If there be omnipotence in the stroke, there is omnipotence in the recoil." That is, every word is a word spoken *again*, or against again; there would be no words otherwise. Since recoil and aversion have been expressed at any time only by breathers of words, mortals, their strokes may be given now, and may gather together now – in a recoiling – all the power of world-creating words. The sentence introducing the three just cited asserts: "Man also is part of [Fate], and can confront fate with fate." That is, I will now say, Emerson's way of confronting fate, his recoil of fate, is his writing, in every word; for example in every word of "Fate," each of which is to be a pen stroke, a common stroke of genius, because a counter stroke of fate. You make your breath words in order not to suffocate in the plenum of air. The power he claims for his words is precisely that they are not his, no more new than old; it is the power, I would like to say, of the powerlessness in being unexceptional, or say exemplary. ("We go to Herodotus and Plutarch for examples of Fate; but we are examples.") This unavoidable power of exemplification may be named impressionability, and seen to be responsibility construed as responsiveness, passiveness as receptiveness.

These are various ways of looking at the idea that the source of Emerson's conviction in what I called the objectivity (I might have called it the impersonality) of his prophesying, his wing-reading and omen-witnessing, lies in his writing, his philosophical authorship, a condition that each of his essays is bound to characterize and authenticate in its own terms.

A characteristic of this authorship is announced in the opening paragraph of the quite early "Self-Reliance": "In every work of genius we recognize our own rejected thoughts; they come back to us with a certain alienated majesty." Even from those who remember this sentence, there is, I have found, resistance in taking Emerson to be naming his own work as an instance of the work he is characterizing, resistance in taking that sentence about rejected thoughts as itself an instance of such a rejected thought coming back in familiar strangeness, so with the power of the uncanny. The mechanism of this rejection and return is, I suppose, that characterized by Freud as transference, a process in which another person is magnified by our attributing to him or to her powers present in our repressed desires and who, putting himself or herself aside for a moment, gives us useably what we have shown ourselves unusefully to know. It is an interpretation of Kant's mechanism of projection that he calls the sublime, reading our mind's powers in nature, in the air. Emerson's authorship enacts, I have gone on to claim in the most recent work I have been doing, a relationship with his reader of moral perfectionism in which the friend permits one to advance toward oneself, which may present itself, using another formulation of Emerson's, as attaining our unattained self, a process which has always happened and which is always to happen.

The word "majesty" reappears in "Fate," again in a context in which the presence of a "thought and word of an intellectual man . . . [rouses] our own mind . . . to activity": " 'Tis the majesty into which we have suddenly mounted, the impersonality, the scorn of egotisms, the sphere of laws, that engage us." A "sphere of laws" into which we have suddenly mounted, as if attaining a new standpoint, suggests Kant's Realm of Ends – call it the eventual human city – in which the reception of the moral law, the constraint, as Kant names the relation, by the moral imperative, expressed by an "ought," is replaced by the presence of another, like and unlike myself, who constrains me to another way, another standpoint Kant says (Emerson says, transfiguring Kant, a new standard); this other of myself – returning my rejected, say repressed, thought – reminds me of something, as of where I am, as if I had become lost in thought, and stopped thinking. In "Experience," Emerson expresses finding the way, learning as he more or less puts it, to take steps, as to begin to walk philosophically, in the *absence* of another presence – more accurately, in allowing himself to present himself to the loss of presence, to the death of his young son.

His description of his authorship in that essay takes the form – I have given my evidence for this elsewhere – of fantasizing his becoming pregnant and giving birth to the world, to his writing of the world, which he calls a new America and calls Being. In "Fate" he is giving the basis of his authorship in that passage about riding alternately on the horses of his private and his public nature. Those are descendants of the horses he invokes, in his essay on "The Poet," in naming the Poet as one whose relation to language is such that "In every word he speaks he rides on them as the horses of thought." The idea is that the words have a life of their own over which our mastery is the other face of our obedience. Wittgenstein in *Philosophical Investigations* affirms this sense of the independent life of words in describing what he does as "leading words back from their metaphysical to their everyday use," suggesting that their getting back, whatever that achievement is, is something they must do under their own power if not quite, or always, under their own direction. Alternating horses, as in a circus ring, teach the two sides of thought, that objectivity is not a given but an achievement; *leading* the thought, allowing it its own power, takes you to new ground.

The achievement of objectivity cannot be claimed for oneself, that is, for one's writing. As in "Self-Reliance": "I would write on the lintels of the door-post, *Whim*. I hope it may be better than whim at last." But in the necessity for words, "when [your] genius calls [you]," you can only air your thoughts, not assess them, and you must.

In Emerson's as in Wittgenstein's way of thinking, ethics is not a separate field of philosophical study, but every word that comes from us, the address of each thought, is a moral act, a taking of sides, but not in argument. In Emerson's terms, the sides may be called those of self-reliance and conformity; in Wittgenstein's terms, those of the privacy and emptiness of assertion he calls metaphysical, and the dispersal of this empty assertiveness by what he calls leading words home, his image of thinking. It strikes me that the feature of the intersection of Emersonian with Wittgensteinian thinking that primarily causes offense among professional philosophers is less the claim to know peculiar matters with a certainty that goes beyond reasonable evidence (matters like the location of the Deity's side, or of the temptation to insistent emptiness); and less the sheer, pervasive literary ambition of their writing; than the sense that these locations, diagnoses, and ambitions are in service of a claim to philosophical authorship that can seem the antithesis of what philosophical writing should be, a denial of rational or systematic presentation apart from which philosophy might as well turn itself into, or over to, literature, or perhaps worse.

The worse one may call esotericism, an affect it seems clear to me both Emerson and Wittgenstein recognized in themselves. Wittgenstein recognizes it in his continuous struggle against his interlocutors, whose role sometimes seems less to make Wittgenstein's thoughts clearer, than to allow him to show that his thoughts are *not* clear, and not obviously to be *made* clear. They must be *found* so. Emerson recognizes his esotericism in such a remark from "Fate" as: "This insight [that] throws us on the party of the Universe, against all and sundry . . . distances those who share it from those who do not." But what is the alternative? At the close of "Experience" Emerson suggests that the alternative to speaking esoterically is speaking polemically (taking sides in argument), which for him, as for Wittgenstein, gives up philosophy, can never lead to the peace philosophy seeks for itself. (The philosopher I am reading who preceded Emerson in contrasting something like the esoteric with the polemical in considering the presentation of philosophy, as a matter internal to the present state of philosophy, is Hegel.) The dissonance between these thinkers and professional philosophers is less an intellectual disagreement than a moral variance in their conceptions of thinking, or perhaps I can say, in their concepts of the role of moral judgment in the moral life, in the way each pictures "constraint."

If slavery is the negation of thought, then thinking cannot affirm itself without affirming the end of slavery. But for thinking to *fail* to affirm itself is to deny the existence of philosophy. It is accordingly no more or less certain that philosophy will continue than that human self-enslavement will end. Philosophy cannot abolish slavery, and it can only call for abolition to the extent, or in the way, that it can call for thinking, can provide (adopting Kant's term) the incentive to thinking. The incentive Emerson provides is just what I am calling his authorship, working to attract our knowledge that we are rejecting, repressing thinking, hence the knowledge that thinking must contain both pain and pleasure (if it were not painful it would not require repression; if it were not pleasurable it would not attract it).

The linking of philosophical thinking with pain is expressed in an Emersonian sentence that seems a transcription at once of Plato and of Kant: "I know that the world I converse with in the city and in the farms is not the world I *think*" ("Experience," last paragraph). To think this other world, say the Realm of Ends, is pleasure; to bear witness to its difference from the actual world of cities and farms is pain. Here, perhaps, in this pleasure and pain, before the advent of an imperative judgment, and before the calculation of the desirable, is the incentive of thinking that Kant sought. The pain is a function of the insight that there is no reason the eventual world is not entered, not actual, hence that I must be rejecting it, rejecting the existence of others in it; and the others must be rejecting my existence there.

I note that it is from here that I would like to follow on with Emerson's understanding of the origination of philosophy as a feminine capacity, as following his claim, toward the end of "Fate," that I excerpted earlier: "The truth is in the air, and the most impressionable brain will announce it first, but all will announce it a few minutes later." He continues: "So women, as *most* susceptible, are the best index of the coming hour. So the great man, that is, the man most imbued with the spirit of the time, is the impressionable man" – which seems to divine that the great man is a woman. The idea that philosophical knowledge is receptive rather than assertive, that it is a matter of leaving a thing as it is rather than taking it as something else, is not new and is a point of affinity between Wittgenstein and Heidegger. Emerson's thought here is that this makes knowledge difficult in a particular way, not because it is hard to understand exactly, but because it is hard to bear; and his suggestion, accordingly, is that something prepares the woman for this relation to pain, whereas a man must be great to attain it. I grant that this may be said stupidly. It may be used – perhaps it most often is, in fact – to deny the actual injustice done to actual women. Must it be so appropriated? By philosophical necessity? But I associate Emerson's invocation of the feminine with a striking remark of Hélène Cixous's, in which she declares her belief that while men must rid themselves of pain by mourning their losses, women do not mourn, but bear their pain. The connection for me here is that the better world we think, and know not to exist, with no acceptable reason not to exist, is not a world that is *gone*, hence is not one to be mourned, but one to be borne, witnessed. The attempt to mourn it is the stuff of nostalgia. (In the closing paragraph of "Experience" I remember: "Patience, patience, we shall win at the last." I had not until now been able to understand this as the demand upon Emerson's writing, and his readers, to let the pain of his thoughts, theirs, collect itself.)

Is philosophy, as Emerson calls for it – we must keep reposing the question, without stopping it – an evasion of actual justice? It hasn't kept Emerson from sometimes writing polemically, as his West Indies and his Fugitive Slave Law addresses attest. His direct idea, to repeat, is that polemic is an evasion, or renunciation, of philosophy. How important a loss is the loss of philosophy?

I think sometimes of Emerson, in his isolation, throwing words into the air, as aligned with the moment at which Socrates in the *Republic* declares that the philosopher will participate only in the public affairs of the just city, even if this means that he can only participate in making – as he is now doing – a city of words. As if without the philosopher's constructions, the actual human city would lack not alone justice in fact, but would lose the very concept, hence the imagination, of justice. Whether you think keeping that imagination alive is a valuable activity depends on how you think the reign of justice can come about.

I began in effect by saying for Emerson that the loss of philosophy is the loss of emancipation – of the imagination of the possibility of emancipation as such – from all forms of human confinement, say enslavement. I make explicit now, again, for a moment the thought about thinking that I claim is implicit throughout Emerson's writing (not solely in "Fate," however painfully there) – the thought that human freedom, as the opposition to fate, is not merely called for by philosophical writing but is instanced or enacted by that writing: the Emersonian sentence is philosophical in showing within itself its aversion to (turning away in turning toward) the standing conformation of its words, as though human thinking is not so much to be expressed by language as resurrected with it.

Let us accordingly transfigure once again: "In the history of the individual there is an account of his condition, and he knows himself to be party to his present estate." The days of the individual are told, counted out, in his condition by the words he suffers, and in his estate by the statements he utters: to know himself, as philosophy demands – or say to acknowledge his allegiances – is to take his part in each stating and in each silence.

In my encounter in 1983 with the essay "Fate," I did not speak of Emerson's philosophical authorship and esotericism, and I did not see the connection between Emerson's mode of thinking and his moral perfectionism, his constraint of his reader through his conviction in the magnified return of the reader's own rejected thoughts. It is as if in my desperateness to show Emerson capable of rigorous, systematic thinking, against the incessant denial of him as a philosopher, I felt I could not at the same time show his practice of thinking as one of transfiguring philosophy, in founding it, finding it, for America. I could not, as it were, *assume* his right to speak for philosophy. My primary focus in my earlier encounter with "Fate" is on Emerson's use of the term "condition," and his relation of it to the term "terms" (meaning words and meaning stipulations) and the term "dictation," which I claim shows Emerson turning the *Critique of Pure Reason* on itself, taking its fundamental term "condition" in its etymological significance as speaking *together*, so suggesting that the condition of the possibility of there being a world of objects for us is the condition of our speaking together; and that is not a matter of our sharing twelve categories of the understanding but of our sharing a language, hence the task of philosophy is not the deriving of privileged categories but of announcing the terms on the basis of which we use each term of the language. Any term may give rise to what Wittgenstein calls a grammatical investigation, but beyond "condition" and its relatives, my earlier essay got just to the idea of "character" as, as always in

Emerson, meaning the fact of language as well as the formation of an individual. But even that distance allowed me to summarize the essay's word as saying that character is fate, that the human is fated to significance, to finding it and to revealing it, and – as if tragically – fated to thinking, or to repressing thinking. Emerson – the American who is repeatedly, famously, denied the title of philosopher and described as lacking the tragic sense – writes an essay on freedom entitled "Fate" and creates the mode of what we may perhaps call the tragic essay.

If I now add the use of the word "constitution" in the essay "Fate" to the terms whose terms I demand, Emerson's claim for his philosophical authorship becomes unpostponable. Along with "condition" and "character," other philosophical terms Emerson allows the reader to find unobtrusive are "possibility" and "accident," and "impression" and "idea." "Constitution" appears in "Fate" only a few times, but its placement is telling, and the essay's array of political terms or projects magnifies its force: I cited earlier the term "resolution"; and we have heard of our being party to our estate; and then a not notably obtrusive sentence speaks of "this house of man, which is all consent, inosculation and balance of parts" – where "consent" works to associate "balance of parts," with "checks and balances," and "house" thus names each of the branches of Congress. Here is an example of what I called placement:

> Jesus said, "when he looketh on her, he hath committed adultery." But he is an adulterer before he has yet looked on the woman, by the superfluity of animal and the defect of thought in his constitution. Who meets him, or who meets her, in the street, sees that they are ripe to be each other's victim.

In my earlier essay I read this as the claim that most of what we call marriage is adultery, not a thought original with Emerson. Now, according to my implied hypothesis that every metaphysical claim in "Fate" about freedom, and its deprivation, is to be read also in a social register, as applying also to the institution of slavery, I read the phrase "the defect of thought in his constitution" to refer to the famous defect in the Constitution of the United States concerning those persons who are, let's say, interminably unfree, a defect which adulterates our claim to have established a just and tranquil human society, corrupts it, makes it spurious. I'll come back in a moment to the passage I mean.

From at least as early as "Self-Reliance" Emerson identifies his writing, what I am calling his philosophical authorship, as the drafting of the nation's constitution; or I have come to say, as amending our constitution. When he says there, "No law can be sacred to me but that of my nature," he is saying no more than Kant had said – that, in a phrase from "Fate," "We are law-givers," namely to the world of conditions and of objects, and to ourselves in the world of the unconditioned and of freedom. But the next sentence of "Self-Reliance" takes another step: "Good and bad are but names readily transferable to that or this; the only right is what is after my constitution; the only wrong what is against it." (The anticipation of Nietzsche's genealogy of morals is no accident.) Such a remark seems uniformly to be understood by Emerson's readers so that "my constitution" refers to Emerson's personal, peculiar physiology and to be the expression of his incessant promotion of the individual over the social. Such an understanding refuses the complexity of the Emersonian theme instanced in his saying that we are now "bugs, spawn," which means simultaneously that we exist neither as individual human beings nor in human nations.

The promise that we are capable of both is the fervent Emersonian theme to the effect that each of us is capable of speaking what is "true for all men." This capacity Emerson envisions in endless ways, often as speaking with necessity (a transfiguration of what philosophers, especially of what Kant, means by necessity). The theme is fervently announced in Emerson's various formulations of the vision that the innermost becomes the outermost: In "The American Scholar": "[The scholar] is one who raises himself from private considerations and breathes and lives on [as if they were air] public and illustrious thoughts"; in "Self-Reliance": "To believe your own thought, to believe that what is true for you in your private heart is true for all men – that is genius" – and specifically it is that which in every work of genius comes back to us with the alienated majesty of our own rejected thoughts. Speaking what is "true for all men," what in "Fate" Emerson speaks of as "truth com[ing] to our mind," is the event of insight he describes as "throw[ing] us on the party and interest of the Universe . . . against ourselves as much as others." – "[Throwing us] on the party . . . of the Universe," – as if to say taking its part (as if taking sides with the Deity) – puts me in mind of what Kant calls "[speaking] with the universal voice," which is the essential feature in making an aesthetic judgment (going beyond a mere expression of individual taste), namely that it demands or imputes or claims general validity, universal agreement with it; a claim made in the face of the knowledge that this agreement is in empirical fact apt not to be forthcoming. Moral judgment also speaks with – or rather listens to – what we might call the universal voice, in the form of the capacity to act under the constraint of the moral imperative, the imperative of the universal (of the universalizable). Emerson is, I am suggesting, appealing to something of the kind in simply claiming as a fact that we can, in thinking generally, judge the constitution of the world and of the lives complicitous with it from a standpoint "all and sundry" may be expected to find in themselves. The great difference from aesthetic and moral judgment is that the constitutional judgment demanding the amending of our lives (together) is to be found by each of us as a rejected thought returning to us. This mode of access to what I am calling constitutional judgment seems to me no less well characterized by Emerson than moral or aesthetic judgments are by philosophers generally. (If Emerson's "representativeness," his universalizing, is not to go unexamined, neither should his habitually condemned "individualism." If he is to be taken as an instance of "humanism" (as if he doesn't really mean much definite by being "thrown" on "the interest of the Universe") then he is at the same time to be taken as some form of anti-humanist, working "against ourselves," against what we understand as human (under)standing.)

It is the appeal to what we have rejected, as it were forgotten, say displaced, that gives to Emerson's writing (and to Wittgenstein's) the feel of the esoteric, of work to whose understanding one is asked to convert. It is an obvious sign of danger for professional, university philosophy, and it should be. Emerson ought to have to make his way, to bear the pain of his arrogating his right to speak for philosophy in the absence of making himself curricular, institutionalizable, polemical. Which is another way of saying that it does not follow from his institutionalized silencing that he has failed to raise the call for philosophy and to identify its fate with the fate of freedom. The fact of his call's repression would be the sign that it has been heard. The apparent silence of "Fate" might become deafening.

The absoluteness of the American institution of slavery, among the forms human self-enslavement takes, hence the absoluteness of philosophy's call to react to it, recoil from it, is announced, as I have more or less said, in the sentence cited earlier from the West Indies address: "Language must be raked, the secrets of the slaughter-houses and infamous holes that cannot front the day, must be ransacked, to tell what negro-slavery has been." I take the idea of raking language as another announcement, in a polemical context, of Emerson's philosophical authorship, of what cannot be undertaken polemically.

A surface of the idea of raking language is a kind of Emersonian joke, namely that we are to respond to the fact, be responsible to it, that the largely unquestioned form or look of writing is of being raked on a page, that is, raked in parallel straight lines; and then to recognize that bringing what writing contains to light, letting these words return to us, as if to themselves, to mount suddenly to their majesty, to the scorn of egotisms, is to let the fact of them rouse our mind to activity, to turn it to the air. Perhaps we are to think that the fact of language is more telling than any fact uttered within it, as if every fact utters the fact of language: against this fatedness to language, to character, against, that is, what I earlier called our condemnation to significance, it figures that it is we who are raked. To think of language as raking and recoiling, is to think of it, though it may look tranquil, as aimed and fired – at itself, at us – as if the human creature of conditions, fated to language, exists in the condition of threat, the prize of unmarked battles, where every horizon – where the air of words (of what might be said) gravitates to the earth of assertion (of what is actually said) – signifies a struggle between possession and dispossession, between speech and silence, between the unspeakable and the unsilenceable. (Here I am letting myself a little express, as earnest of wishing to describe better than I can, the anguish I sense in Emerson's language in "Fate.")

The particular direction in the raking of language I emphasize now is its office in *telling*; which is to say, in counting and recounting – "[telling] what negro-slavery has been" is how Emerson put it – hence in telling every enslavement. An origin of the word "raking" is precisely the idea of reckoning, of counting, as well as recking, paying attention. Of the endless interest there may be in thinking of language itself as a matter of counting, I confine attention momentarily here to the connection between counting or telling and the writing of the American constitution.

When in the second paragraph of "Experience" Emerson asks, bleakly, "How many individuals can we count in society?," he is directing our attention back, wherever else, to the famous paragraph containing what I earlier quoted Emerson as calling "the defect of thought in [our]constitution." That famous paragraph is the fifth – it is also just the fifth sentence – of the Constitution of the United States: "Representatives and direct Taxes shall be apportioned among the several States which may be included within this Union, according to their respective Numbers, which shall be determined by adding to the whole number of free Persons, including those bound to service for a Term of Years, and excluding Indians not taxed, three fifths of all other Persons." The paragraph goes on to specify the calculation of democratic representation, and I find the comic invoking in "Fate" of the new science of statistics, in its attention to populations, to be another allusion to the "defect," the lack of philosophical necessity, in our constitutional counting. In the large we do not see how many we are; in the small we do not know, as Emerson puts it in "The American Scholar," whether we add up to what the "old fable" calls "one Man." As if we do not know whether any of us, all and each, count. We are living our skepticism.

So again, Emerson's simultaneous use of the idea of "my constitution" – his transfiguration of these words – so that we know they name at once his make-up and the make-up of the nation he prophecies, is a descendant of Plato's use of his *Republic* – his city of words – to form a structure at once of the soul and of its society. That is part of my cause in finding Emerson's philosophical prose, his authorship, to earn something like Plato's description (a city of words) for itself – as I find Thoreau's *Walden* to do – hence to imagine for itself the power to amend the actual city in the philosophical act of its silence, its power of what Emerson calls patience, which he seeks as the most active of intellectual conditions. (Even one who recognizes this possibility of his or her own constitution as entering into an imagination of the constitution of the just city may find no city even worth rebuking philosophically – through the proposal of a shared imagination – but purely polemically. This condition may sometimes be pictured as a form of exile rather than of Emerson's agonized membership. Yet it is not clear how different these forms are. I have elsewhere identified Emerson's idea of American membership, his philosophical stance toward America, as one of immigrancy.)

Nothing less than Emerson's peculiar claim to amendment would satisfy my craving for philosophy. But nothing so much creates my fears for it. I am aware that I have mentioned the name of Heidegger once or twice in these remarks, but cited no word of his. And yet in my present return to Emerson's "Fate" and my sense of its tortured, philosophical silence about the tyranny of the institution of slavery – in its effort, as I have more or less put the matter, to preserve philosophy in the face of conditions that negate philosophy – I am aware of a kind of preparation for some explicit coming to terms on my part with Heidegger's relation with the tyranny of Nazism, an explicitness I have, with growing discomfort, postponed over the years. Here is motivation for the present essay I cited at the outset. It is to pose for myself the following questions: Am I prepared to listen to an argument in Heidegger's defense that he was, after his public falling out of favor with the regime, attempting to preserve philosophy in the face of conditions that negate philosophy? If not, how am I prepared to understand, as in his 1936 lectures on Nietzsche and in his contemporaneous "Origin of the Work of Art," his call of a people to its historical destiny, and his announcement of a form of the appearance of truth as the founding of a political order? Such questions press me now not alone because of the oddly late and oddly stale recent accounts of Heidegger's extensive involvements with Nazism, and the inundation of responses to these revelations by so many of the major philosophical voices of Europe, but because of the pitch to which my sense of Nietzsche's absorption in Emerson's writing has come, and of Heidegger's absorption or appropriation, in turn, of Nietzsche.

Only some three years ago did I for the first time read all the way through Heidegger's sets of lectures on Nietzsche, delivered from 1936 to 1940, surely the most influential interpretation of Nietzsche to have appeared for serious philosophers in Europe. Emerson's presence in Nietzsche's thought as Heidegger receives it – in certain passages of Nietzsche that Heidegger leans on most heavily – is so strong at certain moments that one has to say that Nietzsche is using Emerson's words; which means that Heidegger in effect, over an unmeasured stretch of thought, is interpreting Emerson's words. Here are two instances: in volume II of the English translation of the Nietzsche lectures, Heidegger notes that Nietzsche's "early thought . . . was later to become the essential center of his thinking." Heidegger mentions two school essays of Nietzsche's and in a footnote the translator notes in passing that the essays exhibit the "influence" of Emerson, and quotes two sentences from the longer of the essays, "Fate and History: Thought":

> Yet if it were possible for a strong will to overturn the world's entire past, we would join the ranks of self-sufficient gods, and world history would be no more to us than a dream-like enchantment of the self. The curtain falls, and man finds himself again, like a child playing with worlds, a child who wakes at daybreak and with a laugh wipes from his brow all frightful dreams.

Compare this with a sentence from the next to last paragraph of "Fate": "If we thought men were free in the sense that in a single exception one fantastical will would prevail over the law of things, it were all one as if a child's hand could pull down the sun." Nietzsche is not "influenced" by Emerson but is quite deliberately transfiguring Emerson, as for the instruction of the future. This happens early and late. In the section from Book III of *Thus Spoke Zarathustra* called "The Convalescent," of which Heidegger's reading is among the high points of his opening set of Nietzsche lectures, Nietzsche says this: "To every soul belongs another world; for every soul, every other soul is an afterworld." In Emerson's "Fate" we find: "The hero is to others as the world." The relation of transfiguration here is the clearer the more one goes into what Emerson means by the hero (who is in principle every soul) and into his view of how souls touch.

So I am faced with the spectacle of Heidegger's in effect – unknowingly – facing certain of Emerson's words, guiding himself in these fateful years by signs from, of all places on earth, the waste of America. How do I guide myself? Do I guide myself by the thought that since Emerson is the philosopher of freedom I can, in his mediation through Nietzsche to Heidegger, in principle trust to our eventual success in showing Heidegger's descent into the allegiance with tyranny to be an aberration – hence redeemable – of his philosophical genius? Or must I guide myself instead by the thought, that since Heidegger is so radically, unredeemably compromised, and since Emerson is mediated by philosophers of the powers of Nietzsche and of Heidegger, it is not even to be trusted that we will eventually succeed in showing Emerson's genius to be uncompromised by this mediation, so that the way of philosophy I care about most is *as such* compromised?

# What Did Derrida Want of Austin?

What I have chosen to present here is roughly the middle third of the middle chapter of a small book I am trying to finish under the title *A Pitch of Philosophy*, representing work I think of as exploring scenes of the human voice in autobiography (where the voice is searched for, or stolen); in philosophy (where voice is arrogated, hence essentially arrogant); and in opera (where it is absolutely expanded, is perhaps incarnated or perhaps disembodied, and, in women, mostly, is ended). Instead of speaking of scenes of the human voice, I might rather say scenes of the encounter of the ordinary and the metaphysical voice, which is roughly to say, of the human and the inhuman voice. (Down the road, in the placing of skepticism, these considerations should lead to a sense of the male philosophical voice repressing the female voice in itself.) In what follows I have not tried to remove all traces of this context, especially not of the autobiographical, which threads through the chapters. How much of what I have excerpted will communicate itself, I of course do not predict. An ideal result, from my point of view, is that the material will seem familiar – some of you, I know, are more familiar with some of Derrida's writing than I am – but that the light I try to bring to it will show the landscape of issues it discovers still to contain some surprises.

In a brief memoir I published a few years ago of my teacher J. L. Austin – the purest representative of what came to be known as ordinary language philosophy – I spoke of the revelatory effect his first classes had on me, when he came from Oxford to Harvard for the spring term of 1955 to deliver the William James Lectures on performative utterances (entitled *How To Do Things With Words*). Like any conversion experience – any turning, however small, of a cheek, of a mood – the effect is apt to seem out of proportion to anything you might think to call its cause. Conversion (or as Emerson says it, aversion) is of its nature hard to explain, to others as to oneself. Could it really be that so decisive a change in the course of my life – let's even say it was merely, or only, or sheerly, or just, or simply (favorite distinctions of Austin's) a change in my intellectual or academic ambition or craft – could this have been brought about by Austin's trivial, if amusing examples? *How* could it have been? (I think of the difference between shooting your donkey by mistake or by accident; of the difference between being sure and being certain of a color; of seeing bread and seeing the signs of bread; of our asking "How do you know?" not "Why do you know?," and of our asking "Why do you believe?" but in general not "How do you believe?") Austin's teaching was the occasion for me on which to ask, somehow differently from any way in which I had been able to ask it before, whether I was *serious* about philosophy – not quite as measured by its importance (either to the world, or to my society, or to me), but as measured by a question I felt a new confidence in being able to pose to myself, and which itself posed questions, since it was as obscure as it was fervent. It presented itself as the question whether I could speak philosophically and mean every word I said. Is this a sensible test in choosing a career? Is it sensible even in choosing – or seeing that you have chosen – a friend? And does it mean that I have – before I speak – to ask whether I am sincere in my words, whether I want all of their consequences, put to no matter what scrutiny? Who would say *anything* under such conditions?

It is against such a perplexity that I take up a discussion of Austin first published by Jacques Derrida in 1971, entitled "Signature Event Context." Some would call it an attack; others a sort of celebration or homage. It became famous in America a few years later among literary theorists, and known to some philosophers, when it was translated into English and published together with a reply by John Searle, a philosopher trained at Oxford while Austin was still alive and whose book on the theory of speech acts has been and continues to be far more influential – in both literary studies and in philosophy – than Austin's original work that invented the subject.

Derrida has recently republished his side of the exchange with Searle, under the title *Limited Inc*, together with yet another substantial set of reactions to those events. It has more than once been said that this encounter between Derrida and Austin, and then, at much greater length, between Searle and Derrida, represents the closest that the traditions of French–German philosophy and American–English philosophy have come to talking to one another in detail. I hope this isn't the closest, but I am not prepared to argue against it now. It is, though, my impression, with respect to a different, related, conversation, between related traditions of scholarship and thinking – namely between those of philosophy and of literary studies – that the encounter between Derrida and Austin and then Searle has proved to have done more harm than good. The effect of Searle's reply has encouraged the suspicion (to say the least) in which Derrida's work continues to be held by many, I think most, professional philosophers in the English-speaking world of philosophy; and Derrida's influence within literary studies has kept the image of Austin too much tethered to his theory of performatives, and, within that theory, to the several citations Derrida found suitable to his own purposes for "Signature Event Context."

This has helped perpetuate the thought that Austin underwrites some idea that language contains a general, unified dimension of effect that can be called one of performance, and that he advances a general contrast between ordinary language and literary language. These ideas alone are sufficient to destroy any contribution Austin's distinctiveness might lend in such discussions.

My own feeling is that while Derrida found Austin philosophically interesting, even congenial, and Searle had found Austin useful and worth defending against *this* treatment, neither really felt that Austin's is a philosophical voice whose signature it is *difficult* to assess and important to hear out in its difference. If what either of them says about Austin's ideas of language is right, then my question of seriousness, forced upon me by those ideas, is not only difficult to articulate, but pointless. This is a way of putting the drift of my original defense of Austin, in 1957, in the first essay I published that I still use, the title essay of *Must We Mean What We Say?* – so far as that was pertinent to the analytical (American–English) tradition of philosophy, a tradition which Searle, in a later moment, also claims to speak for. To show this sense of pointlessness, or failure to hear Austin's difference, in the opposing case of Derrida – from the French–German side of the philosophical mind – is not something I have tried before now, for lots of reasons. None of them, I think, is as important as a complex reason for now going ahead to try it, namely that while the notoriety of this exchange has significantly been a function of Derrida's fame, and I suppose of his studied indecorousness toward Searle's dismissiveness; and while many people now, I believe, express relief that Derrida's influence is receding; that influence remains immeasurably powerful and, on my view, deserves a grander fate than its detractors wish for it, if perhaps not quite the dominance that its admirers have traded on.

But there is a more substantive reason for taking up Derrida's discussion. He is right to have emphasized the fundamental importance of the human voice in Austin's work, and his "Signature Event Context," read so as to elicit answers from Austin's work – not as a criticism of it that is either to be accepted or rejected, either as omnipotent or as incompetent (which have mostly been the options taken in my hearing) – constitutes an acute and rare encounter concentrated on the interacting themes of voice, writing, and philosophy.

So that now, and here, I would find it unbecoming of me not to say what I can directly about Derrida's encounter with my old teacher. I shall proceed in a sense with deviousness, but in a sense with maximum directness. To outflank what for my purposes would perhaps be unnecessary and certainly exhausting engagements, I am going to pretend that the controversy between Derrida and Searle did not happen – as in a sense each of them insists it did not; and speak to Derrida's words (some of them) on Austin as if for the first time. How far this fiction can excuse me for my ignorance of so much else of Derrida's writing is a threatening question for me. I risk it, since any light I can offer on this encounter must come from Austin's way of taking things, and it seems to me that that way remains of more interest than I find generally taken in it at present.

The first third of the chapter in question here – a portion I am skipping – sketches out various significant intersections between Derrida's procedures and those of the ordinary language philosophers (including, within the territory of this argument, the later Wittgenstein along with Austin). That first third proposes Austin's and Wittgenstein's originality in the way they take up the cause of what they call the ordinary against what I have described as philosophy's metaphysical flight from the ordinary – you might say, from finitude. Derrida, and the, or a, Continental tradition of philosophy more generally, grant an autonomy – institutional and intellectual – to metaphysics as a persistent structure of Western thought, or inner menace of it.

The strains of analytical philosophy seek precisely to revoke this grant – logical positivism in favor of the tests of science and logic, Austin and Wittgenstein in favor of what they call the ordinary. These traditions (what I am here calling the Continental and the analytical) are set to seem hopelessly naive, even quite senseless, to one another. (In the work of Austin and of the later Wittgenstein the concept of the ordinary is developed specifically in contrast to what they sense as metaphysics – or I might rather say, in contrast to that philosophical skepticism against which what Wittgenstein calls metaphysics takes its stand: the ordinary for them *is* what skepticism denies (hence in a sense invents).) Yet both traditions are genuime possibilities of philosophy now.

I might roughly align the traditions in this way. Derrida sees ordinary language as an effect of a general writing which is its possibility. Wittgenstein sees metaphysics as an effect of ordinary language (needing its words but denying their shared criteria). Each pivotal concept at issue between Derrida and Austin (presence, writing, voice, word, sign, language, context, intention, force, communication, concept, performance, signature, not to mention, of course, consequent ideas of philosophy, analysis, the end of philosophy, fun, work) is turned by their differences. I know of no position from which to *settle* this systematic turning.

I note that I will be taking for granted in what follows here that these thinkers, i.e., Derrida and Austin:

1  share the object of dismantling the metaphysics of Western philosophy;
2  find philosophical procedures that are neither those of commentary nor of interpretation nor of refutation, but ones of what Derrida calls *going through* texts; and specifically
3  going through exemplary texts, exemplary of their respective traditions, in order

4    to produce an exemplary text in response; and specifi-
     cally one meant
5    to show how to think in the aftermath of some
     *destruction* of thinking.

I have in mind in these latter points specifically Derrida's
*Speech and Phenomena*, on major texts of Husserl's;
and Austin's *Sense and Sensibilia*, on A. J. Ayers's *The
Foundations of Empirical Knowledge*. One might put the
task of showing thinking in the aftermath of thinking as
showing how to assert importance or seriousness in the
repudiation of our established ideas of importance and of
seriousness.

Given these intersections, I ask: How is it that Derrida
misses the extent of Austin's differences from the classical
and/or academic philosophers with whom Austin, as much
as Derrida, is at odds? It is that the differences at some
stage stop seeming important? If the philosophical mind of
the West has divided itself into mutually shunning traditions, then each is bound to determine its own idea of
philosophical importance.

The eventual refusal of Austin's difference is all the
more surprising since in "Signature Event Context"
Derrida pays Austin an unusually handsome, complex,
compliment, calling his analysis of performative utterances (i.e., the work of *How To Do Things With Words*)
"patient, open, aporetical, in constant transformation, often more fruitful in the acknowledgment of its impasses
than its positions" (p. 14). These precious predicates are
doubtless awarded by Derrida out of a recognition of
specific further affinities his work has with Austin's. Both
are philosophers of what may be called limitation, both
interested in the morality and politics of speech (out of
something like a shared sense that concepts, without the
most scrupulous attention, impose, and are imposed,
upon us), and both take the struggle against metaphysics
as a struggle for liberation, for something more than rea-

son, as it were, itself. Most specifically, there is an appreciation of the fact that Austin's analysis of the performative may be seen to be motivated precisely as an attack on what deconstruction attacks under the name logocentrism.

I take logocentrism – I speak hesitantly and use phrases from *Speech and Phenomena* – to name a "limitation of sense to knowledge, of logos to objectivity, of language to reason" (p. 99), amounting to "the unity of thought and voice in logos" (p. 74), from which Husserl had at once started and stopped an effort at "the emancipation of speech as nonknowing" (p. 97). (I once put what I gather to be a congenial thought by formulating an intuition I find insisted on by thinkers from Emerson to Wittgenstein to the effect that our fundamental relation to the world is not one of knowing.) Austin refers to his sense of this limitation as "the descriptive fallacy," though he objects to the name, and describes the fallacy in the opening sentence of the second paragraph of *How To Do Things With Words* as follows: "It was for too long the assumption of philosophers that the business of a 'statement' can only be to 'describe' some state of affairs, or to 'state some fact,' which it must do either truly or falsely."

Austin's so-called theory of speech acts is in effect the presentation of a massive class – or set of classes – of counter-examples to this assumption – a set that proves to have interests well beyond this intial interest – namely one in which what are grammatically statements are *not* in the business of stating facts truly or falsely. Opening instances, or classes of instances, of such (performative) counter-examples are (I remind you, quoting Austin): "I do," "I name this ship the *Queen Elizabeth*," "I give and bequeath my watch to my brother," "I bet you a dollar it will rain tomorrow." Austin comments: "In these examples it seems clear that to utter the sentence (in, of course, the appropriate circumstances) is not to *describe* my doing of what I should be said in so uttering to be doing, or to *state* that I am doing it: it is to do it. None of the utterances cited is either true or false: I assert this as obvious and do not argue it" (p. 5, p. 6).

By the deflationary phrase "not the *business*" (of all "statements") Austin comes as close as he can to saying, in Derrida's terms, "not [the] internal and positive condition of possibility [of language]" ("Signature Event Context", p. 17). Derrida was bound to be drawn to Austin's discoveries. But when he says that "Austin was obliged to free the analysis of the performative from the authority of the truth *value* . . . and to substitute for it at times the value of force, of difference of force (*illocutionary* or *perlocutionary force*) . . . which is nothing less than Nietzschean" ("Signature Event Context", p. 13), I find that Derrida's sense of the matter is something like the reverse of mine. There is a Nietzschean line in Austin, but at another angle, which I shall want in a moment to measure.

Derrida does not recognize – or attach particular significance to – Austin's argumentative move, taking performatives as counter-examples to a philosophical thesis, as, whatever else, a specific and (then) current counter to logical positivism, specifically to positivism's notorious claim that utterances other than statements are lacking in a measure of rationality, or say adequation to reality. Such utterances – for example, judgments of aesthetics, of ethics, and of religion – were held by these philosophers to contain a brand of meaning inferior to that enjoyed by verifiable statements, namely so-called emotive meaning as opposed cognitive or scientific meaning, and were held therefore as unamenable to a (further) philosophical assessment. When Derrida interprets Austin as "[substituting] . . . at times the value of force . . . for the value of truth," this directly negates, destroys, Austin's counter to positivism, which *depends* upon an understanding of the performative utterance as *retaining* an adequation to reality (to certain factual conditions) equal to that of verifiable statements. Which is to say that

Austin's work in the theory of performatives is designed precisely to retain "the value of truth."

We might say that what Austin "substitutes" at the place of a concept of truth is *not force but "felicity."* Statements, if adequate to reality, are true; if not, false. (This defines the concept of a statement.) Performatives, if adequate to reality, are felicitous, if not, then, in specific ways, infelicitous.

It might seem to make more sense to say that what Austin substitutes "force" for is not truth but meaning. But this description rather fits what logical positivism does in assigning to non-statements emotive as opposed to cognitive meaning – so even this substitution would again hand Austin over to a critical enemy. (It could be said that Austin's distinction between utterances with illocutionary force and those with perlocutionary force – the former doing something *in* saying something, the latter doing something *by* saying something; the former identifiable as performatives, the latter as some, if you like, undefined sorts of performances – is designed precisely to counter positivism's sense of a uniform brand of meaning or of force attaching to non-statements.)

I cannot stop here to verify these claims. Nor is it possible now, briefly, to recreate the climate in which positivism was pervasive and dominant in the Anglo-American academic world from the mid-1940s through the 1950s and beyond, almost throughout the humanities and the social sciences, a hegemonic presence more complete, I believe, than that of any one of today's politically or intellectually advanced positions: positivism during this period was virtually unopposed on any intellectually organized scale. No publication was more successful in popularizing logical positivism – no work of academic philosophy was itself more popular, or more cited and required in philosophy courses – than A. J. Ayers's *Language, Truth, and Logic.* Austin's antagonism toward

Ayers's *Foundations of Empirical Knowledge* was in long preparation.

Misplacing the role of "force," Derrida takes the role of "felicity" and "infelicity" to be one of determining failures of language as external to language rather than as conditions of language's possibility – an insight he thinks Austin misses. He describes Austin as "rejecting", "deferring", or "excluding" a " 'general theory' [that would interrogate] as an essential predicate . . . the value of risk or exposure [of language] to infelicity." Derrida cites two instances of what he evidently takes to be an exclusion of one and the same such theory. But in the passages Derrida cites from Austin's text there is the exclusion (if that is the word) of *two different* theories. The first theory considers performatives as actions; the second considers them as utterances. The first theory deals with, in Austin's terms, "extenuating circumstances" applying to all *actions*; the second deals with what Austin describes as parasitical uses or non-serious uses of any *utterance*.

Evidently Derrida was not aware that these are each theories that Austin had developed elsewhere: the former is the theory of excuses (one of Austin's most notable contributions to philosophy), the latter is his theory of pretending or imitation (I'll sometimes refer to it as a theory of insincerity) (which is one of Austin's *least* notable contributions – by his own account). So that when Austin says he is "excluding" the theories from his discussion, the obvious sense is that they are simply not being rehearsed in this place; it follows that they are not going unmentioned or unalluded to, or excluded or deferred or rejected, as Derrida insists. So what? One cannot read everything. How costly in this instance was Derrida's unawareness (if I am right in inferring it) of this work of Austin's beyond *How To Do Things With Words*?

It might not have been so costly had Derrida taken up the appearance, in the opening chapter of that book, of the citation – uniquely there in Greek, as if calling attention to itself – from Euripides' *Hippolytus*. Not that any other reader I know of *How to To Do Things With Words* stops to wonder about it either. (Notably not Shoshana Felman in her admirable and admiring book-length reading of it. This deserves a discussion of its own.) One can perhaps understand why. It seems to make no sense to say that deliberately superficial, witty, mocking Austin, would be inscribing the relation of his work on performative utterances to the realm of the tragic. (Just as it seems to make no sense that cheerful Emerson captured the imagination of the theorist of tragedy, Nietzsche – so no matter how often you hear of Nietzsche's all but incessant transcriptions of Emerson's sentences, or perceive it, you *cannot* for very long remember it.)

What is the connection of Austin's theories of excuses and insincerities to the idea or fact of tragedy?

Excuses are as essentially implicated in Austin's view of human action as slips and over-determination are in Freud's. What does it betoken about human action that the reticulated constellation of predicates of excuse is made for it – that human actions can be done unintentionally, unwillingly, involuntarily, insincerely, unthinkingly, inadvertently, heedlessly, carelessly, under duress, under the influence, out of contempt, out of pity, by mistake, by accident, etc., etc.? To experience Austin's meticulous journey through his world of concrete examples of these qualifications – and scores of others – is momentarily to put aside all question of how we know such things, or whether to know them is philosophy. Excuses betoken, we might say, the incessant, unending vulnerability of human action, its exposure to the independence of the world and the preoccupation of the mind. I would like to say that it turns philosophy's attention patiently and thoroughly to something philosophy would love to ignore – to the fact that human life is constrained to the life of the human body, to what Emerson calls the giant I always take with me. The law of the body is the law.

Who, such as Austin, would dwell on excuses endlessly who did not surmise that the consequences, concomitants, up-shots, effects, results, etc. of the human necessity for action, and of action for movement – the body a parchment of its displacements – did not surmise that the necessity for action is apt to become unbearable? (Who but one familiar with despair would so fight for joy – like Emerson and after him Nietzsche?) Excuses mark out the region of tragedy, mark it as the beyond of the excusable, the justifiable, the explainable, (the sociable?). Who among philosophers has a theory of forgiveness, and whether it is giveable? It must be a theory of comedy.

This route to the sense of the unbearableness of human action – of its overdetermination or its overindebtedness, as of the unreachableness of justice – is a kind of interpretation of Nietzsche's perception of Hamlet's lethargy. This is the point at which I predicted a Nietzschean element will bear on Austin's work. The point is rather disguised in Austin's comments on the citation from the *Hippolytus*, and I myself did not for a long time understand this with sufficient seriousness.

Austin at that moment is combatting his mortal philosophical enemy, or one of its recurring faces, the craving for profundity. (This characteristically goes in Austin with a questioning of philosophy's intellectual seriousness. But the other faces of philosophy's enemy are marked in nothing short of the endless list of his terms of criticism of other philosophy.) The question of profundity arises here in Austin's deflecting of a charge against his view that it is superficial, or, as he puts the charge here, "flippant." The charge is that his view, according to which saying something is sometimes doing something, really comes to claiming that "To marry is to say a few words" or "Betting is simply saying something" (p. 7). Austin goes on to try lessening the sound of flippancy by emphasizing the importance of specific circumstances in the uttering of performatives, but soon his diagnosis of the sense of his superficiality darkens.

I quote most of two paragraphs, both to suggest how immeasurably complex the issues are that we are tracking here in a few strokes, and to mark that on the pivot of profundity we have turned to the second of the two general doctrines that Derrida turns out to charge Austin with excluding from his discussion of performatives. The first, the doctrine of excuses, to repeat, takes up the failures performatives share with all actions; the second is the doctrine that takes up the failure performatives share with all utterances, the doctrine of pretense or insincerity or seriousness:

> But we may, in objecting [on the ground of apparent superficiality in the suggestion that doing something is merely a matter of saying some words], have something totally different, and this time quite mistaken, in mind, especially when we think of some of the more awe-inspiring performatives such as "I promise to. . . ." Surely the words must be spoken "seriously" and so as to be taken "seriously"? This is, though vague, true enough in general – it is an important commonplace in discussing the purport of any utterance whatsoever. I must not be joking, for example, nor writing a poem. But we are apt to have a feeling that their being serious consists in their being uttered as (merely) the outward and visible sign, for convenience or other record or for information, of an inward and spiritual act: from which it is but a short step to go on to believe or to assume [without realizing] that for many purposes the outward utterance is a description, *true or false*, of the occurrence of the inward performance. The classic expression of this idea is to be found in the *Hippolytus* (1. 612), where Hippolytus says . . . "My tongue swore to, but my heart (or mind or other backstage artiste) did not." Thus "I promise to . . ." obliges me – puts on record my spiritual assumption of a spiritual shackle.

It is gratifying to observe in this very example how excess of profundity, or rather solemnity, at once paves the way for immorality. For one who says "Promising is not merely a matter of uttering words. It is an inward and spiritual act" is apt to appear as a solid moralist standing out against a generation of superficial theorizers: we see him as he sees himself, surveying the invisible depths of ethical space, with all the distinction of a specialist in the *sui generis*. Yet he provides Hippolytus with a let-out, the bigamist with an excuse for his "I do" and the welsher with a defence for his "I bet." Accuracy and morality alike are on the side of the plain saying that *our word is our bond*. (pp. 9–10)

When Austin later "excludes" this sort of material from (further) discussion, he flags it hurriedly, in the passage Derrida in fact cites:

Secondly, as *utterances* [vs. as actions] our performances are *also* heir to certain other kinds of ill, which infect *all* utterances. And these likewise, though again they might be brought into a more general account, we are deliberately at present excluding. I mean, for example, the following: a performative utterance will, for example, be *in a peculiar way* hollow or void if said by an actor on the stage, or if introduced in a poem, or spoken in soliloquy. This applies in a similar manner to any and every utterance – a sea-change in special circumstances. Language in such circumstances is in special ways – intelligibly – used not *seriously* [my emphasis, J. D.] [Austin had twice put it in scare quotes, S. C.], but in many ways *parasitic* upon its normal use – ways which fall under the doctrine of the *etiolations* of language. All this we are *excluding* from consideration. Our performative utterances, felicitous or not, are to be understood as issued in ordinary circumstances. ("Signature Event Context", p. 16)

(When Hippolytus says "My tongue swore to, but my heart did not" is he an actor on a stage? Does he think he is, that is, take himself to be on some inner stage? Does

Austin imagine one or other of these possibilities to be in effect? Does Austin think we, or anyone at any time, may not be able to tell these differences? Or not tell them in the case of Hippolytus because we cannot tell them in ourselves? Is there something in the figure of Hippolytus that would confuse Austin about all this? (His slam at the "back-stage artiste" suggests that there is.) I am trying not to let such questions take over.) Derrida introduces this block of quotation in the following way:

> The second case of this exclusion concerns our subject more directly. It involves precisely the possibility for . . . every . . . utterance . . . to be "quoted." . . . [Austin] insists on the fact that this possibility remains *abnormal, parasitic,* that it constitutes a kind of extenuation or agonized succumbing of language that we should strenuously distance ourselves from and ignore. And the concept of the "ordinary," thus of "ordinary language," to which he has recourse is clearly marked by this exclusion.

Derrida's saying "the second case of this exclusion" and, after the quotation, his speaking of "the whole general theory" seems obviously to be taking Austin to be excluding one theory twice rather than invoking two separate theories.

But what the doctrine of excuses does for cases of extenuation, Austin's work represented in his paper "Pretending" in part does for, and is meant eventually to do more for, cases of etiolation, parasitism, and in general the realm of the "non-serious"; it is the place in which pretending is linked with, and initially defined so as to be distinguishable from, feigning or posing as, affecting or shamming, mimicking or merely imitating, rehearsing or acting. I said that Austin was not satisfied with this beginning; I recall his saying that he had been led to publish it prematurely. (That is itself a vignette that speaks to differences between the traditions of philosophy in their theories and institutions of publishing.)

I should say that I do not imagine such a doctrine of pretending, however corrected and extended, doing for cases of the non-serious what excuses do for cases of extenuation. To glimpse why, I ask, comparably to the question I asked about excuses, what it betokens about utterance or about action that they can suffer, say, imitation (to take that title for the iterative). It betokens, roughly, that human utterances are essentially vulnerable to insincerity (you may say false consciousness) and that the realization that we may never know whether others are sincere or genuine (I do not exclude the first person) is apt to become unbearable. (We might say that it returns philosophy's attention to the fact that human life is constrained to the life of the mind, such as it is.) The reason for my lack of confidence in Austin's theory of pretence to uncover such matters is that the family of concepts associated with it is one that contrasts with the knowledge or the reality or genuineness of action as a whole, a contrast that arises in skepticism with respect to minds at the place that the possibilities of dreaming and hallucination and illusion arise in skepticism with respect to things; and Austin's survey of that site is compatible with the view, or enforces it, that philosophical skepticism *cannot* be a serious intellectual stance, that it is, let us say, parasitic on the serious. So that Austin is philosophically apt to be impatient with the sense that it may be harder to detect a difference between the genuine and ungenuine in speech than to assess the need for the extenuation of an action.

I have criticized Austin's views at length on such a ground, and this is no time to outline the fateful importance I attach to his rejection of the threat of skepticism, or say his exclusion of it. What is at stake is not simply an exclusion but a theory of exclusion, or a place for one, and a theory at the same time of seriousness. It takes non-seriousness to be a declaration of self-exclusion (as if Iago, and not Othello, is the image of the skeptic). This is dangerous political terrain. Is the implication that to be non-serious is to be be a parasite? Is it chance that this sounds like a criticsm famously levelled at Weimar intellectuals?

That such criticism is dangerous, and is pertinent to Austin's work, is inscribed by Austin in a startling diagnosis he gives of philosophy's institutionalized dismissal of the "subtlety, complexity, and diversity" of ordinary words. I refer to a sentence in the introductory chapter to *Sense and Sensibilia*: "It is essential, *here as elsewhere* (my emphasis), to abandon old habits of *Gleichschaltung*, the deeply ingrained worship of tidy-looking dichotomies" (p. 3). Rather than demanding exclusion, Austin is evidently here struggling against it, indeed against the most famous of the historical nightmares of exclusion, the Nazi policy of coordination, elimination of "untidy-looking" differences. Is Austin serious in assigning, however rhetorically, philosophy's organizational requirements to a wish for fascistic mastery?

Austin first offered the lectures in question in 1947. His experience in World War II in British Intelligence concerned with German affairs was known to have left various traces in his later life. Am I making too much of it? Let's be reasonable and ask what Austin proposes to *do* about seriousness, I mean how he envisions shaping people up. Is it, after all, however rhetorically, to call the police? *Is* this what the order in ordinary language comes to? – an obsession with the proper, with property, with propriety? Where is the fun in that – which is something Austin claimed to be returning to philosophy?

What does Austin do? To "dismantle a doctrine" is what at the end he implies he has wished to accomplish. But my question is still: How does whatever he does constitute a criticism of unseriousness? I assume it is by exemplifying seriousness, evidently of some new, or renewed, kind.

Might this mean exemplifying thinking and writing that mean everything they say? And would this mean exhausting or reducing the possible significance of each of their marks? To be extent these pictures makes sense, I think we are bound to say they make no sense. I would like to say that Austin's exemplification of seriousness takes the form of showing that he can listen. This is hardly an original claim for philosophy. It is as immediate a description of the moral of the dialogue form, as it is of the more familiar claim of philosophy to argumentative acumen, a point demonstrated most vividly in our era by Wittgenstein's *Investigations* with its continual fragments of dialogue. The claim to listen is apt to be insufferable (especially – perhaps – when it is true but restricted, as in Austin's case). And Austin has suffered the consequences – or so I understand the current near-oblivion into which his name has fallen, except for the work on performatives.

Against the background of tragedy, Derrida would not, it seems to me, have been able to dismiss Austin's sense of the relation of voice to writing as he does.

He likes Austin's theory of performatives for its refusal of the view of language as the transferring of a something called a meaning from one place to another (communicating) place. And he likes Austin's instinct in relating writing to speaking by way of the idea of the signature. But then he finds Austin to revert to the philosophical traditon – to which Derrida says he knows of no counter-instance – according to which the authority of meaning resides in the voice (as its intention, its consciousness of, its presence to, a word), and according to which writing is a medium of *extending* that self-identical something of meaning in principle throughout a homogenous semantic space, a realm presumably no less extensive than all of physical space. Austin had written: "Where there is not a reference to the person doing the uttering then in fact he [may be] 'referred to' . . . in written utterances . . . by [tethering] his signature [to it]." This seems reasonably banal. It is meant as devastatingly banal. But Derrida reads it as follows: "Not only does Austin not doubt that the source of an oral utterance in the present indicative active is *present* to the utterance and its statement . . . but he does not even doubt that the equivalent of this tie to the source's utterance is simply evident in and assured by a *signature*." ("Signature Event Context", p. 19)

To look past the banal here is, in terms used earlier, precisely to assume that what is in question is a metaphysical tie from a metaphysically original source to a metaphysically unique signature – which is precisely to beg the question of Austin's claim to the ordinary, which, to repeat, he invokes in contrast not to the literary but to the metaphysical. Austin, it is true, has no theory of the origin of the metaphysical, of the human restlessness in the ordinary and its attraction to the beyond, not to mention the before. Wittgenstein can be said to have such a theory: it lies in his identification of our wish for super-concepts joined by super-connections in a super-order as the result of a process (inherent in philosophy) of what he calls subliming our language; Hume more casually calls it speaking "intensely." (Wittgenstein may accordingly be labelled a philosopher of metaphysical language as accurately as a philosopher of ordinary language. Neither label, aimed at him, is accurate without the other.)

On my view of Austin's and Wittgenstein's work, they understand skepticism and metaphysics as forms of intellectual tragedy. I might accordingly frame a question I have for Derrida about his sense of Austin's phantasy of the tethering signature in this way: Does Derrida take Austin to propose a solution to the unassurance and opacity of the speech depicted in, for example, Euripides' *Hippolytus* by in effect inviting us tragic or skeptical characters to sign our utterances? – so in effect proposing the turning of tragedy into farce?

This is particularly hard to entertain against the backdrop of the *Hippolytus* since that play may be thought of precisely as a tragedy of sincerity, that is to say of *the inability to be insincere,* an inability *not* to be signed on to your words and deeds. (This may be taken as the founding or presenting question of Thoreau's thinking.) Hippolytus triples the tragedy of his step-mother Phaedra by his inability to break his promise, his promise to the nurse not to tell (what her telling him has caused) that he knows or knew of Phaedra's ungovernable passion for him. Phaedra's inability to keep her passion to herself in the first place may suggest calling this play also a tragedy of expressiveness, or of the desire for intelligibility (further links of tragedy with moral necessities). And I find no good reason in reading Austin to take him otherwise than as supposing that every ill or farce that can attend the voice can affect the signature.

The Greek sentence Austin calls classic and cites from Euripides and translates as "My tongue swore to, but my heart did not," is Hippolytus's reply to Phaedra's nurse when she reminds him of his oath to keep her revelation a secret. Austin uses this distinction between tongue and heart as a type of the philosophical use of profundity (call it metaphysics) to exempt yourself, or exclude yourself, from the everyday responsibilities or accountabilities that make civilized life possible – giving an out to bigamists, welshers, con artists of every stripe. But Austin himself seems to be forgetting something about the *Hippolytus*, since he apparently attributes the line to Hipplytus as a species of excuse, whereas Hippolytus never uses it so, and indeed the pity and terror involved are some function of the knowledge that the most *casual* of utterances may be irretrievable: so my tongue swore without my heart – *nevertheless I am bound.* In rejecting Hippolytus's glimpse of a profundity in making a promise – in speaking as such – Austin says, as noted: "Morality and accuracy alike are on the side of the plain saying that *our word is our bond.*" But this overlooks the fairly blatant fact that on Hippolytus's view of promising, the saying that our word is our bond proves a fatal *curse.* (Hippolytus's anti-type is Don Giovanni, for whom apparently no word is binding. It is as if Austin, uncharacteristically, does not keep his difference between tethering and bonding. Neither does Derrida, who also does not – as Austin does – suggest the difference between these relations and that of *shackling*, to which Austin attributes a claim be calls "spiritual" and mocks.)

(I leave open the matter of explaining Austin's "forgetting" of so signal a fact about the *Hippolytus*, that its title character never breaks his word. This is surely tied up with a fact that is too ecstatic in its possibilities not to mention but whose specific implications I am still looking for time to follow out – including some explanation of how I had until recently all but forgotten it – namely the fact that the very line Austin quotes and calls "classic" is also quoted in Plato's *Symposium* (as well as in his *Theatetus*, as well as in Aristophanes' *The Frogs*). Socrates in the *Symposium* cites it about half way through the text, as it becomes his turn to speak, using it specifically as an excuse, and specifically as one which he happily and ironically thereupon gives over, but an excuse to get out of speaking rather than one to get out of keeping silent. So Austin was evidently quoting and inscribing at least the *Symposium* as much as the *Hippolytus*. Can one not want to know why? My immediate guess as to what Austin wanted to forget is that the saying of words is not excusable the way the performance of actions is, or in a word, that saying something is after all, or before all, on Austinian grounds not exactly or merely or just or quite or transparently doing something.)

Derrida's diagnosis or interpretation of writing "that is proper and peculiar to philosophy" ("Signature Event Context," p. 3) is of "an iterative structure cut off from all absolute responsibility, from *consciousness* as the ultimate authority, orphaned and separated at birth from the assistance of its father, [which] is precisely what Plato condemns in the *Phaedrus*" (ibid. p. 8). Philosophy sees that writing is meant for the absent receiver/addressee, who may be dead. It *fails* to consider, according to

Derrida, that it works equally in the face of the death of the sender/addressor. Taking Condillac as his instance, Derrida writes: "The absence of the sender . . . from the mark that he abandons, and which cuts itself off from him and continues to produce effects independently of his presence and of the present actuality of his intentions, indeed even after his death, his absence, which moreover belongs to the structure of all writing . . . of all langauge in general . . . *this* absence is not examined by Condillac" ("Signature Event Context", p. 5). A direct philosophical conclusion seems to be that absolute responsibility for an essential predicate cannot be tethered to a mortal. What other brand of responsibility can there be?

Perhaps I was too hasty all those years ago – in discovering Thoreau's *Walden* as a scripture, a testament, that is, written in anticipation of his own death – when I refused to allow that this was an acknowledgment, or theory, of all writing. Such a claim seemed to me not to capture Thoreau's achievement, not to distinguish it from, say, the making of a will (a notable form of words), which is about as common as possessions. (I might now say that the writing of a testament in view of one's death is a description of all *serious* writing.) This aside, let's look at the fit of this description of writing with Austin's idea of tethering. I read Austin not as denying that I have to abandon my words, create so many orphans, but as affirming that I am abandoned *to* them, as to thieves, or conspirators, taking my breath away, which metaphysics seeks, as it were, to deny. (Emerson's emphasis on writing and thinking as self-abandonment is on my mind here.) Hence Austin's tethering reverses Derrida's picture of philosophy's concept of writing as *extending the limits* (or "relaxing" them ("Signature Event Context," p. 3)) of the voice or breath (as if *that* much is too obvious to Austin to mention); turns it so to speak into one of *limiting the inevitable extension* of the voice, which must always escape me and will forever seek its way back to me. (I may say here that I primarily do not know whether Derrida takes the idea of *Limited Inc* here to stake a claim to know or to say something about limitation or about incorporation or about ink that Austin has missed.)

Say then that the price of having once spoken, or re-marked, taken something as remarkable (worth noting, yours to note, about which to make an ado), is to have spoken forever, to have entered the arena of the inexcusable, to have taken on the responsibility for speaking further, the unending responsibility of responsiveness, of answerability, to make yourself intelligible. It is in recognizing *this* abandonment to my words, as to unfeasible epitaphs, presaging the leave-taking of death, that I *know* my voice, *recognize* my words (no different from yours) as mine.

Doubling an earlier question about the bearability of action, of having a body, in relation to the action of tragedy, if we now ask, How is it that having a voice or signature is bearable, a voice that always escapes us, or is stolen?; and, What is the nature of the force that allows language not only to mean and to state but to perform and to suffer?; these begin to sound like questions of opera.

# Seminar on "What Did Derrida Want of Austin?"

The following is a transcription, revised in December 1993, of the seminar held at Bucknell University on May 5, 1993. The participants included Professors Marianna Archambault, Paul Archambault, Richard Fleming, Pauline Fletcher, Peter Fosl, Gary Grant, James Heath, John Murphy, Kathleen Page, Michael Payne, Jean Peterson, John Rickard, Harold Schweizer, Gary Steiner, and Frank Wilson.

**OPENING REMARK** It's a pleasure to welcome Stanley Cavell to this seminar, and we thank the rest of you very much for joining us. I thought we might best begin by asking Professor Cavell perhaps very briefly to outline the major points he made last night in his paper "What Did Derrida Want of Austin?," so that we'd have some reminder of the common ground that we share. We can then proceed to ask him questions about his presentation.

**CAVELL** Thank you. I'll try.

My idea was to take up a controversy that has been on the academic stage for some time and the fact of which, and the effects of which, when I would from time to time be made aware of them, could make me feel quite miserable – effects specifically concerning Austin's currency and usefulness, and, more generally, ones concerning the possibility of useful trades across the rift between the German–French and the English–American traditions of philosophy. Derrida's "Signature Event Context" came to my attention when its translation was published together with John Searle's reply to it, and then Derrida's reaction in turn to that reply, in the opening two numbers of *Glyph*, in 1977, some six years after its appearance in French. I read through these texts with various emotions, but eventually with dismay. I had begun making my way through Derrida's *Grammatology*, with alternations of excitement and of perplexity, and sensing the causes of his notoriety. In the case of "Signature Event Context" I felt both that he understood something in Austin that others missed and also that he was not interested in something else in Austin which I regarded as fundamental. Searle's reply seemed to me – what should I say? – not exactly unexpected; but when Derrida proved to be so enraged by it (you could call it amused, but *that* amused?) it made me wonder about Derrida's stake in responding to Austin. If you unquestionably admire Derrida then his theatrical response to Searle can seem hilarious and devastating, high intellectual slapstick. But you are not apt to be just charmed if you are a pupil of Austin's, with cause for gratitude to him, a record of some criticism of him, and if when you read the original exchange you were already aggrieved at the stinginess of response to his gifts for philosophy. Originally I was not prepared to take the exchange as quite my business. Then when Derrida reprinted his part in it a couple of years ago, plus a new response, in a volume entitled *Limited Inc*, edited by Gerald Graff, I concluded that the issue was still in motion and found myself in any case impelled to have some public say. To do so, I picked up from something both Searle and Derrida declare, or mock, that an encounter between them, and what they represent, never or only questionably happened, and enact the fiction that I am encountering Derrida's "Signature Event Context" on my own, as for the first time. But to do this means to me to enact, what is for me not a fiction, the awkwardness of the absence, to my knowledge, of exemplary encounters of the two traditions of Western philosophy with one another.

In the cases of Derrida and of Austin, we have figures each of whom takes himself as representative of, or a product of, a more or less coherent tradition of thinking within which their own views are marginal or eccentric. Each of them writes as present to something that is to be undone. (And to imagine these revolutionaries asking, What Is To Be Undone? is to imagine them answering, Everything.) Dismantling is sometimes Austin's word for what he has to do, a word obviously in the line of the word deconstruction. Dismantling has in it, as deconstruction does, the idea of leaving or putting all the elements of a text, as it were all the original pieces, in play. Neither thinker is out merely to destroy, or deny. (Wittgenstein does say in the *Investigations* that he comes in a sense to destroy something; but I didn't go into that in the selection of material I read last night, and I won't raise it here.) Sheer destruction of a kind may be the outcome of their work (say the complete vanishing of interest in certain forms of question, or obsession), but the process of the destruction has to be a philosophical one; it is not the destruction of an army or of a city which, as Wittgenstein articulates his fantasy of destruction, as it were leaves behind it a landscape of ruin. Philosophers are not kings. If the philosophers destroy, it is – as Thoreau puts the matter at the opening of *Walden* – with the work of their hands only.

Unexpected as Derrida's encounter with Austin may appear, it was no accident. They bear deep features in common. There is, for example, the concern of each with philosophy's, or thinking's, or writing's limitations, and their necessities, or habits; there is an awareness of the moral dimension and of political dimensions of language; and they are quite at one in their attack on what deconstruction calls logocentrism, the thing Austin calls the descriptive fallacy. And they each bring a certain fun into philosophy. If you do not like them you do not like their fun; if you do like them it is in part for the fun. Derrida (accordingly) appreciates and pays Austin an extremely handsome set of compliments, finding him patient, methodical, more interesting at the impasses of his argument than in whatever he thinks to be the thesis or conclusion of his arguments. High compliments coming from Derrida. I suppose I set up the encounter of Derrida with Austin this way to show that it occurs well past any encounter that he and Searle could have had. (This is no explanation of why the encounter they had took the specific form it has.)

Another specific feature Derrida likes about Austin is his denial that meaning is a kind of corpuscle, as it were, that passes unchanged from one place or origin, through a communicating medium, to another place or destination. And he likes it that Austin attends to the signature. Moreover I say that Derrida is right, all but uniquely among Austin's readers, in pinpointing the feature of the importance of the human voice in Austin. This is a feature of fundamental importance in my understanding of Austin's work. But then of course Derrida has a formidable array of axes designed to discourage certain attentions to the human voice, or to some voice, in the wrong, that is in a metaphysical, way. (I note here, though the bulk of my discussion of the matter in my full paper on Derrida and Austin is omitted here, that the distinction between the metaphysical and the ordinary voice is of the essence for me, as it is in my *The Claim of Reason*. However unclear and uncertain this distinction is, and perhaps must remain, it is critical to see that Austin and Derrida are both to be seen as "against" the metaphysical voice, or against their different characterizations or pictures of such a thing.)

So the question for me becomes: Why does Derrida not see the way in which Austin is at odds as much with his tradition as Derrida is with his tradition? How is it that this connection never takes place for Derrida, or not, for my taste, sufficient, theorized place?

One way to think about this is to note that the way Austin draws differences does not make differences for Derrida. That would hardly be surprising. In foreign territory you sometimes just cannot hear a change of vowel. You may perhaps not see that one bowl is an object of great and telling beauty and a similar one is mediocre. While I do imply that Derrida hasn't an ear for, or patience for, certain dimensions of Austin, for example, for his allusiveness, his seriousness, his mockery of false seriousness – and why or how should he have? – this is not a charge against Derrida's reading that I spend much of my time spelling out. The charges – if that is what they seem to be – that occupy my time are rather simpler ones. First, that Derrida had not read certain texts of Austin that are inscribed in the text he concentrates on, namely in and on Austin's notes on performative utterances, *How To Do Things with Words*; second, that he neglects the inscription of tragedy in that text, Austin's citation from Euripides' *Hippolytus*.

Take the issue of the *Hippolytus* first. It is just the sort of gesture you would expect Derrida to go to town with; as you would in the case of a reader like Shoshana Felman, whose fascinating and important book on Austin's *How To Do Things* also, I believe, does not notice it. And yet it is the gesture in which Austin draws the most pointed moral against those who will fail to take his discovery of performativity with due seriousness, those he accuses of obtuse and devious profundity. Remember how extraordinary as readers Derrida and Felman are. If readers of such powers overlook Austin's gesture, this must have to do with a sense of Austin as, let's say, incapable of bearing up under the consequences of his inadvertent and unguarded seriousness. (I know there are those who deny that Derrida is a powerful reader of philosophical texts, perhaps the same ones who deny this of Heidegger. This symptomatic denial calls for attention on its own.)

About my second charge against Derrida, that he simply hadn't read certain texts presupposed by *How To Do
Things with Words*, I don't see that there should be much
doubt about this. Derrida says, and emphasizes, that there
is a theory that Austin is essentially excluding from consideration. But Austin says that there are two theories in
question; and when he says he is excluding them, as a
contingent convenience, from the present discussion his
quite open meaning is that he has already discussed them
elsewhere, published them previously (anyway they were
both published within a year or so of the time I heard the
lectures on performatives, at Harvard in 1956): they are
the theory of excuses in "A Plea for Excuses" and the
theory of imitation or the parasitic or the non-serious in
"Pretending." When in *How To Do Things* Austin says that
the first of these theories is a theory of extenuation, this is
not just one among other names for what excuses do, it is
Austin's name for their work in "A Plea for Excuses." Do
you imagine that if Derrida had read that text he would
have failed to remember this? He took a chance – don't we
all, all the time, necessarily? – that he had enough context
to follow his instinct; but the stimulus was partial. (This
leaves open why the chance was taken with Austin – I
mean both why it seemed feasible and why it seemed
worth the risk.) In Derrida's case this may be particularly
painful to hear because of his own loathing of being hastily
and incompletely read, his being known for saying, in
effect, to his detractors (doubtless, also, in a different tone,
to his students), "Read a little more; it won't hurt you."

And there is hardly less doubt in my mind that Derrida
had not read *Sense and Sensibilia*, for he would have recognized it to be Austin's dismantling of the English empiricist tradition's view of presence. That is what A. J. Ayer's
book *The Foundations of Empirical Knowledge* – which Austin takes, as he puts it, "as chief stalking-horse" – constitutes and represents, an extended defense of the claim that
we know, that is, can be certain of, only what is present to
our senses, and that this presence is the foundation of

empirical knowledge. The concept of presence occurs, at a guess, at least as often in Ayer's book as the concepts of certainty or of sense statement, and it is Ayer's text that Austin chiefly dismantles.

Now Austin pursues this text so mercilessly, anyway relentlessly, that certain philosophers have never forgiven him for it (for the intention if not for the achievement). (It is my view that some of these philosophers were looking for something nameable not to forgive Austin for.) When on Austin's death Ayer succeeded Austin as White's Professor in Oxford, he undertook explicitly to organize a philosophical effort to destroy Austin's influence, which he found deleterious to philosophy. (This is recorded in *A. J. Ayer: Memorial Essays*, Royal Institute of Philosophy Supplement 30, edited by A. Phillips Griffiths.) Thirty years and more later, this plan sounds more aggressive than it might have at the time, while Austin's attack seems, at least to me, less personal than it might have then. Austin was, in many eyes, a forbidding, cold man. He famously gathered the younger teachers of philosophy at Oxford together each week for a session of Austinian exercises, and some of them, some very brilliant young thinkers, chafed under that treatment. But since it is repeatedly said in the Ayer memorial volume that Ayer's claim to honored memory is not as an original philosopher, and at least some of the contributing philosophers concede Austin's originality, what is the struggle for, what is its political significance? My sense, of course, is that it is internal to institutional philosophy, in any culture I know something about, not to want to hear what Austin has to say.

But if it is as obvious to a student of Austin's as I have claimed it to be that the theoretical material Austin is excluding in *How To Do Things with Words* consists of not one but two theories, each of which Austin had treated elsewhere, and signals by quoting himself, why didn't Searle, for instance, point this out? (Perhaps others have done so since that original exchange. It has been some years since I first mentioned the fact in lectures; they have elicited no such information.) Is or was Searle so uninterested in Austin's mind that he hadn't noticed its quoting of itself? Or was he so dismayed by what he took as Derrida's failures to take Austin's points that he didn't care how extensively Derrida had or had not read Austin? I say in my paper that I don't believe Searle cares about either of these philosophers deeply enough for it to matter to him to get this relation very usefully in view, supposing it were practical to try. And I claim that Austin's is a voice of difference that it is important to follow all the way out in its difference. Derrida recognizes significant affinities with the difference, while Searle regards Austin, I believe, as rather careless in what he says about speech acts, however notable his invention of the subject. Searle's book has replaced, or outstripped, Austin in most philosophical, and in all but all, I think, literary circles. My fear is that the Austin–Derrida–Searle–Derrida exchanges have helped confine Austin's reputation, such as it is, to the fate of a few phrases from his work on the performative utterance.

But to say that Derrida did not read certain essentially related texts of Austin says nothing to the much more interesting issues of why he was moved to respond to what he did read. I cite his high compliments to Austin, but are they enough to acount for his draw to Austin? He is right in the affinity he expresses for Austin in the (denial of) communication of (stable, complete, uniform, controlled) meanings, and in the importance of the signature; and right again – and for me most decisively – in his sense of Austin as resting on a claim for the human voice. That Derrida finds this claim to be something that pushes Austin back into the crowd of philosophers, ancient and modern, in his view of the economy of voice and writing, seems to me not to do Austin's originality justice; but *this* disagreement with Derrida is one I find exceptionally profitable to pursue. I take him to be saying, in effect, that *even* Austin succumbs to the lure of voice. But what I think

Derrida is objecting to here is something he was already in flight from, the specter of the ordinary.

Derrida talks recurrently about the ordinary even in this (for him) miniature, twenty-page text, "Signature Event Context." He says that of course he is not denying that there are "effects" of the ordinary, for example – I take it – that we know, and so are not wrong to say, that there are words and signatures and things and animals and persons, etc. In my philosophical unbringing such a concession is familiar from academic skepticism. It matches the moment in which the academic skeptic says *of course* we know that there are tables and pens and hats, etc., *for practical purposes*. But what are these practical purposes? The goals of life? For what purpose do I not know that the earth, or this room, exists? or these hands? or this fire?

**QUESTION** Who are you paraphrasing now?

**CAVELL** Descartes's skeptic. Hume's skeptic. That skeptic says, or takes the tone in which, he cannot shake the knowledge he has discovered in his closet, namely that we can never know with certainty that there are things and other minds, etc. while at the same time he recognizes that when he leaves his isolation, comes out into the company of others, plays backgammon with his friends, that he will forget this terrible truth – as, of course, he knows he should, being a sociable creature who does not crave insanity. Now this gesture, this "for practical purposes I know," is, I claim, a matching gesture of the "of course we know there are ordinary signatures everywhere, everyday" (even though they do not do what philosophers imagine them to do, something like lock a meaning secured by transparent consciousness to the owner of that consciousness). The gestures further the air of implication that there is a something more to do – a further reality to assess, a fullness of certainty to apply – than human beings can compass. (Derrida also denies certain understandings of this "more." Is this my contradiction, or his?) Of course –

so runs the air – I know your signing the check means that it is your signature, not mine; but only for practical purposes; this is no assurance of my tie to a metaphysically independent world. (Is it an assurance, or lack of it, that I am not you?) Now I say that if Derrida had noticed the business about Hippolytus, it would have been harder for him to continue to insinuate that if, or when, we crave such a tie, Austin would wish to satisfy the craving. I assume that Derrida is not going to say that Hippolytus's denial, or apparent denial, that he has made a promise is just the enactment of the failure of promising to bind metaphysically. Whereas for Austin, Hippolytus enacts the claim that a metaphysician – the metaphysician in each of us – will use metaphysics to get out of the moral of the ordinary, out of our ordinary moral obligations. That is what frightens Austin, and draws his philosophical fire. Derrida does not regard metaphysics as, let us put it this way, morally corrupt from the outset. He may think it intellectually moribund, and to lead to a certain political and cultural corruption of Western culture as such. But this takes metaphysics to have institutional and linguistic bases which cannot vanish at the touch of the ordinary; on the contrary, it is bound to swamp the ordinary, to take it under its own protection, or interpretation. Whereas for Austin, metaphysics is from its origin, from each individual current origin of itself, unnecessary, monitorable, correctible.

Was all that a helpful summary of my lecture?

**QUESTION**  I still don't understand exactly the connection between Austin and tragedy that you outline, the significance of that link. Could you tell us a little about that?

**CAVELL**  My question was: Why does Austin at a certain stage invoke Euripides? What he says about Hippolytus is that instead of acknowledging that the ordinary human being's ordinary word is his bond, is binding, is given to another being, Hippolytus wishes (as Austin seems to remember him) to use the fact that he said something without meaning it to excuse his word from the status of a bond: "My tongue swore, my heart did not." This distinction between tongue and heart represents for Austin a metaphysical dodge, or a deviously motivated attempt at one, between saying and intending. Derrida seems to think – quite astoundingly to me – that Austin isn't, or is insufficiently, suspicious of metaphysical appeals to intention. For Austin that appeal may precisely represent moral corruption (as well as, or because it also does, intellectual corruption). Let me offer another example to stress how banal, unrare, hence philosophically even more distressing to Austin, the kind of case is that I understand him to have in mind. During my first years as a teacher, I proposed a good friend to a neighboring department as a candidate for an assistant professorship. Such matters were, to say the least, less open and systematic in those days, and on the strength of the recommendation, with some additional confirmation, my friend was invited to give the usual lecture and discussion. In due course he was accepted by a formal vote of the department and I was thanked for my efforts. Some weeks later he phoned me to say that he had had a positive call from the department but no formal invitation and that his own department was pressing him either to accept a renewal of his present appointment or to allow them to seek a replacement. I asked the chair of the department in question whether a letter of invitation had been sent and was told that it had not been. I said it was my impression that my friend had been told, or been given the equivalent assurance, that the position was his. Yes, that is true, was the reply, but the administration is worried about the small quantity of publication, however high the quality, and wants assurance about that; and he felt he had no real basis on which to give such assurance. When I protested that my friend had taken the department's statement to him that the position was his as amounting to an offer, for which he is awaiting the formalities, I was told, with no little impatience, that he should not have taken it so, since no empirical statement is certain.

**QUESTION**    That's what you mean by the use of metaphysics to try to get out of an ordinary obligation?

**CAVELL**    That is an instance of exactly what I mean. I should add that the chair's hearing himself say this, in the presence of one frozen with disbelief and disapproval, produced a further outburst of impatience, but resulted in the prompt and dutiful dispatch of the letter.

**QUESTION**    Do you mean that the whole dispute between Austin and Derrida is over metaphysical language? What do you oppose to the use of metaphysical language? What is the alternative?

**CAVELL**    For Derrida there is no alternative. What you have to do is, to use an image, as I recall, from Heidegger, to twist free within it, from it. In Austin the metaphysical contrasts with what Austin calls the ordinary. That is what for him the ordinary is. And that is what metaphysics is, the effort to twist free of the ordinary. There is no flat contradiction or mismatch between Austin and Derrida. For Derrida, philosophy and its metaphysical tradition is a powerfully protected subject institutionalized in or by Western culture, in its pedagogy, its sciences, its writing. For Austin it is rather the folly of a band of philosophers, easily distinguishable from serious citizens. Wittgenstein describes what he wishes to destroy in philosophy as, in the established translation I won't quarrel with here, a house of cards, something that will collapse of its own weight. That this perception represents a great weakness in Austin I accept; I have criticized his work at length for its blindness to the depth and power of the issues of skepticism and of metaphysical attempts to contain it. It is not in the same way a limitation in Wittgenstein's later thought, which can be regarded as providing a theory of the drive to metaphysics and of the possibility and necessity of skepticism – as much a philosophy of metaphysics as it is a philosophy of the ordinary.

I do not imagine that the story connecting Derrida and Austin has a surveyable conclusion. These are two masters of their traditions of philosophy, and they seem both to cross one another and not to cross, to attract and repel one another. That seems to me to exemplify the condition of what I can recognize as the philosophical mind at present. It exists in these two, more or less incommensurable, states. I think I know of no one who is equally at home in both. You might take it as another intellectual feature shared by Austin and Derrida that they deny that there is a history of Western philosophy. But what is shared? Derrida would mean that you cannot tell one unified, non-illusory story linking the thoughts of the (and who says?) significant thinkers of the West. Austin would rather mean that the story to be told, if there is one, is a history of folly and fanaticism, as the moderns sometimes described, in their terms of criticism, the ancients. Bacon calls Aristotle a beast; others called the classical philosophers children. There is a history of intellectual dismissiveness. This is perhaps not disturbing if you take knowledge to be defined by progress and definitively by the advent of the new science at the turn of the sixteenth into the seventeenth century. Since I am not of that persuasion, I want to be able to consult both the likes of Austin and of Derrida.

**QUESTION**   May I pick up on exactly what you just said, that you find both Derrida and Austin useful. In your paper it seemed to me that you made one move in your critique of Austin and another in your critique of Derrida but that each might be seen as derived from the other one. For example, your treatment of the Hippolytus passage in

Austin is the kind of emphasis that one might find Derrida making, taking a quotation or a footnote or something that even careful readers previously, or I think you said even yourself previously, had not noticed or placed (and then also read with the implications of the *Symposium* context as well). And what you said about Derrida was that you wished to critique him for his insensitivity to or ignoring of the ordinary, obviously derived from the value of the ordinary for Austin. Now my question here is if you were making use of some Derridian ammunition in dealing with Austin and some Austinian emphasis on the ordinary in dealing with Derrida, is that an indication of your use and your sense of the value of these people? Or was that simply a rhetorical feature of your talk?

**CAVELL**   That's interesting. You're asking how it is that I can help myself to some of each – why it is they don't repudiate each other in my mind to the very extent that I care about each. This is bound to be a risk, to be evaded only rhetorically, for the sake of getting on, until we know how to measure the distances along the rift of philosophical traditions. But you don't have to have Derrida's fields of ammunition to notice a citation from a Greek tragedy sitting there in the middle of Austin's text. Its going generally unnoticed seems significant to me quite beyond its being just the sort of tip or uncharacteristic step that interests Derrida. I suggested that the significance of its invisibility lies in an implied, shared image of who Austin is as a thinker, an image against which it makes no sense that Austin would invoke tragic literature to figure his moral. Austin insists – does he not? – on the superficiality and the commonness of what he appeals to. It is the other side of his insistence that profundity is the deepest thing we have to fear. Or is it perhaps false profundity toward which he recommends fear? And is this the sort of distinction a superficial denizen of the common room should be trusted to perceive? As for using Austin's ammunition of the ordinary, I do not wish to level it particularly against

Derrida. On the contrary, I take his disparagement of the ordinary to bind him to the process of philosophy from which he seeks to win his freedom (not his alone, I believe).

**QUESTION**    Doesn't it often happen in Cavell that he finds himself surprised by the things that people haven't noticed? The thing I'm thinking of particularly is the *King Lear* paper. In the second part of it you spend considerable time and delicate effort being surprised that no one who has written on *King Lear* had noticed, seemed to have noticed, that this is a tragedy of shame. I have to confess to you that I didn't think of it as a tragedy of shame. I do now but I didn't think of it before as a tragedy of shame. Now is that not just a feature of creative reading, good reading, to suddenly discover that there is something absolutely important in this text that you are reading that no one has really noticed before or not in that way?

**CAVELL**    Is this a criticism of me? I would take my recurrent surprises at what good and creative readers do not see as prompting considerations precisely of what good and creative reading is. But I think there is a difference here, one which I may not be able to capture here and now by improvisation.

I assume that we all know that years after first reading a text we care about, something new may dawn, something at that moment having become terribly plain in the text, something that for some reason one is released from being uncreative or unresponsive toward. That is the sort of experience, I believe, that goes into the concept of the masterpiece. It has its humdrum equivalents. I have a lawyer friend who was thunderstruck to realize, twenty years after carrying one, why a brief case is so called. One comes upon such discoveries all the time, with a familiar blend of local chagrin and delight. But sometimes the experience is not local, not confined. I report that in

Austin's class on excuses, certain stories, trivial in the telling (as, for example, the donkey stories in "A Plea for Excuses" designed to separate the senses of doing something "by mistake" and "by accident"), filled me with a sense of, I might say, living the unexamined life, unlocally, unendingly unresponsive to my own experience. As if I were repressing the meaning of my words – and if these words, then any, anytime. Expressing surprise at what Derrida had not noticed was expressing anxiety about my vulnerability to nasty surprises at my self-ignorance, miserably familiar to me. The surprises I report (I said, for example, that I had for years failed to pay sufficient attention to the Hippolytus reference) are of course mostly ones I have recovered from, so that employing examples of discovery or recovery in philosophy is apt to court theater – the feigned innocence of, for example, asking whether we really see *all* of the table in front of our eyes. Let's call it the theater of producing the obvious – a reason, perhaps, that both Austin and Wittgenstein compare metaphysics to magic. I recognize in myself an effort to preserve the moment of magic by producing new examples in the moment. When this fails it fails wretchedly. (And is the innocence in question feigned? Is it, in philosophizing, acted out, or genuinely remembered? I think Emerson and Heidegger are raising such an issue in picturing philosophizing as a condition of having drunk a certain measure of Lethe; Emerson describes the measure as a little too much.)

I seem to be suggesting that there is an obviousness marking the philosophical that is particular to it, and in particular that is not exhausted in the obviousness sought in good or creative reading. Good and patient reading can alert you to notice that shame is under discussion, or avoidance, in the preliminaries of the opening, casual exchanges of *King Lear*, which are accordingly not preliminaries and are casual the way only the customary brutalities of civilized life can be casual. But the obviousness of the error in describing Edgar as "delaying" revealing his presence to his father is not arrived at so; it is a matter of stopping and seeing that you are saying more than you know, imposing a conclusion, blind to the knowledge that what you are shown are scenes of shunning, disguise, avoidance – perhaps to be overcome, hence logically describable as delays, but perhaps not to be overcome, or not in good time. The obviousness of philosophy (Wittgenstein's quasi-technical term for this is perspicuousness) marks the overcoming of, let us say, resistance of some kind. Wittgenstein calls this, sometimes, our bewitchment; philosophers from Plato to Descartes or Emerson and Thoreau speak of our awakening or of our turning around, as from a walking sleep and as from a blocked path. The shock in philosophy's obviousness is present in the Socratic insight that the oracle's praise of him as one than whom none is wiser must mean that he knows he knows nothing that others do not know. And to come into knowledge that everyone is in a position to have is to sense that one has shunned the knowledge, or as Emerson puts the matter, half a century before Freud, that one has rejected one's own thoughts.

Now to mention that brilliant readers do not notice Austin's reference to Euripides is to imply that they do not sense it to be important enough – to Austin – to mention; and I attribute this sense to a fixed imagination of what Austin is capable of thinking; so that to accept the obvious here demands a wholesale revision of this imagined figure.

I do like learning things, and I like providing what might be news, such as that Hippolytus's line that Austin cites is also quoted by Socrates in the *Symposium*. But I like even more hitting upon articulations of how, perhaps, such a fact fits Austin's drift. To accept my articulation (having to do with Austin's invoking in his own prose the relation of comedy with, let's say, seriousness), you can only consult yourself, not expect an independent confirmation, as with news. The matter is wholly between us. But since my interest depends upon circling the obvious, and since people do not like to be told the obvious, people get annoyed with me, or grudge me the work I do. (Perhaps as often as not they say that what they grudge is my manner of doing it. I am of course no judge of the manner.) I imagine that I am giving a reader something; but such a reader feels that I am depriving him or her of something. So we disappoint one another. Overcoming that disappointment – let's say of the fact of our separateness, and say of the difference in our times of insight – remains to my mind a philosophical task.

**QUESTION**   Could I take you to a different subject? You are very interested in tragedy. And I was wondering if you could perhaps explain to us the problem of the representation of suffering in tragedy. Whether there is in this pair of terms an incompatibility. You do seem to trace such a course in your essay on *Lear* where you very beautifully describe the position of the bystander or the audience to be the suffering tragic hero. Suffering and tragedy might not have very much in common actually but they might be very close to each other.

**CAVELL**   Yes. I have not given this enough thought. I might begin by recognizing that not all tales of suffering are tales of tragedy. This doesn't say very much. All tragic tales are tales of suffering, so which tales of suffering are the tragic ones? Which is just to repeat the question of what tragedy is. A familiar way to think about this is to distinguish tragedy from melodrama. I am myself not terribly interested to do that. Usually, I take it, if you distinguish tragedy from melodrama you slight the melodrama side. But it's hard enough to get a good melodrama. Isn't *Macbeth* a melodrama? I have never sought a definition of tragedy, perhaps because I both disbelieve and believe all the theories. No one could be quite free of the idea that tragedy works as a catharsis of pity and terror, and I test such an idea, in my manner, in various ways.

Pity in theater is not much followed out in Aristotle, as I recall, but the idea of politics as being a reponse to fear or terror is something he emphasizes. The philosopher of pity that interests me most perhaps is Rousseau, also a philosopher of theater, including, it goes without saying, the theater of politics. Then there is the characterization of tragedy as inspiring woe or wonder, the phrase from *Hamlet* used by J. V. Cunningham in his little book on tragedy that I remember reading with profit. I have asked whether this is the same wonder in which philosophy is reputed to begin; and I have compared or contrasted wonder with melodrama's signature tableaux of astonishment – another cross with philosophy, as when Descartes is astonished to discover the unprovability of the world's existence.

All of which points to my concern with tragedy (and with melodrama if it fits) as a working out (a tragic working out, if I can put it so) of the problem philosophy discovers as that of skepticism; and vice versa, my concern with skepticism as a working out (an intellectualized working out) of the human being's incessant vulnerability to the consequences of its passions and its actions. Accordingly, I suppose there are two things immediately that I go on in supposing that I am working with a tragic text. One is the victim's unseen hand in his or her own victimization; another, relatedly, is that the blindness in question can be constituted in the most ordinary inattention to one's desires. The classical locus of the treacherous humdrum or familiar is the familial, with its violent banalities of repetitiveness. When society becomes the locus of familiar violence the individual is less believable as the origin of public action than as its victim, a figure of pathos, perhaps hence of melodrama, as in such cases as those of Magwitch, Anna Karenina, Ibsen's Enemy of the People, Stella Dallas. Consider, beyond this, that the concept of the tragic seems to bear internal relations with the concepts of justice and of nature. However valuable the recognition that so much of what we have called natural has been a product of the cultural and the historical, a price of this disparagement of the natural has been the loss of the tragic (hence, I suppose, of the farcical) as a term of public criticism (a loss, in certain forms, of course, well lost).

**QUESTION**   When I read that chapter on *Lear* I'm actually very glad that I read Lacan before I read you. When one reads Lacan one looks for hitching posts which allow you to oversee what you have read. I do something similar to that when I read your texts. I look for places where you make your discoveries.

**CAVELL**   And you have trouble finding them? That of course might be a sign of my failure to write or to think well enough. But it also might be a sign of my best success. Because what I want in writing philosophy – as my remarks on obviousness should suggest – is to show that whatever discoveries are in store, they are not mine as opposed to yours, and in a certain sense not mine unless yours. Which doesn't mean that in writing I am not *doing* something, something for which, the better done it is, the less I should expect credit. No wonder I once or twice wrote about the pain of unacknowledgment.

**QUESTION**   You do in Part Four of *The Claim of Reason* come close to defining tragedy when you say that it's an insistence or a continual insistence to say that which cannot be meant. You talk about the increasing effort to mean something that cannot be meant as a proper conception of tragedy. We narrowly grab on to something or seemingly somehow center on something and then make that the entire issue and we don't look at our whole lives, and that then can produce psychic anxiety and conflicts of a skeptical nature with our ordinary existence.

**CAVELL**   That does seem like what I am hearing myself now say. I've forgotten the context in *The Claim of Reason*.

**QUESTION** It is when you talk about the issues of slavery and abortion in Part Four that you make such statements.

**CAVELL** (I should identify this questioner as a teacher who has just taken a class of undergraduate students all the way through *The Claim of Reason*, something I have never attempted to do.) Yes, there comes a point in philosophy at which the very thing you're insisting on is something you precisely cannot mean, just like that. Does the moment in *The Claim of Reason* help us see how a human being gets into such a situation? And is this illuminated by my location of the concept of tragedy?

I believe, though my evidence for it is mostly second hand, that current views on abortion are debating the question whether those who oppose abortion on the ground that the embryo is a human baby can exactly mean what they say. This was the question put in *The Claim of Reason*, which proposes that, since abortion is abhorrent without the metaphysical claim that the human embryo is a human baby, hence that serious pro-choice advocates can and will know this, abortion may be called for, and should safely and unpunitively be available, in the kinds of serious cases that pro-choice advocates argue for. Since there is no convincing argument against the metaphysical claim of the humanity of the embryo, the convincingness of the proposal rests on the convincingness of the idea that this claim cannot exactly or fully be meant. The convincingness of this idea requires, at a minimum, articulating what is actually meant, and articulating what would have to be meant if the claim were exactly or fully meant, and accounting for the passion that overrides these articulations. Schematically: What is actually meant is that the human embryo is human, not, say, wolf; the issue is whether this adequately accounts for the abhorrence. And what would have to be meant if the claim were exactly meant is that abortion is a crime horrible even beyond most premeditated murder, ranking with Herod's slaughter of the innocents. That many will protest that they do precisely feel this way suggests that we are in a region of tragedy. The sense of tragedy lies not, however, in this apparent disagreement of moral or religious sentiments, but in the lack of transparent necessity in the high incidence of abortion, too often caused by defective social institutions (insufficient and unequal training in prevention of pregnancy, insufficient and inefficient routes to adoption, insufficient and inadequate public child care, etc.). These articulations should clear the way to taking up the question of the passions (and the perhaps sometimes suspicious lack of passion) associated with abortion.

**QUESTION**  In your reading of Lacan, do you read Lacan from the perspective of philosophy? Or do you see Lacan as in some sense doing philosophy?

**CAVELL**  To the extent that I have a good perch in reading Lacan – I'm just a beginner – it is by being impressed by the explicitness of his philosophical claims. After a number of false starts with his work, I took the advice of Shoshana Felman to begin early and move chronologically. (Sound pedagogical advice is of its nature something one may not be able to provide for oneself. From whom may one accept it?) I'm now up to the late 1950s, and there have been sufficient rewards for me to be quite eager for time to go further. In those years, Lacan's references to and readings of philosophical texts are plain and about as frequent as references to and readings of literary, anyway to non-psychoanalytic, texts generally. And the reading strikes me as characteristically interesting, justifiably assured, and pertinent. (It is equally important to my enjoyment of these years of Lacan that analogies to mathematical concepts are mostly still absent.)

Yet Lacan presents himself as a master – hence justified

in anchoring the symbolic of his classroom – within the field of psychoanalysis, not philosophy. So if Lacan is unabashed in his appeal to philosophical texts as themselves usable in his casework within the Freudian structure, then what is psychoanalysis? What kind of institution, to begin with, is a (Freudian) psychoanalytic institute? Let us say that the authority of such an institute – what justifies its political power of credentialing – is a function of its enacting, preserving, and developing the Freudian text. (If the function were that of, in ordinary terms, furthering a science, the relation of psychoanalytic institutes and universities, at least in the United States, would not be as problematic as it is. I should confess my view that the relation of philosophy to universities should seem more problematic than it does.) Now you read in Freud's texts that what is conducted there is not philosophy; but this denial of philosophy is repeated so often by Freud that I become suspicious, on Freudian grounds, and begin thinking that Freud is insisting that, somehow, philosophy is after all his. I suppose this means that psychoanalysis is some specific inheritance (or, as Wittgenstein puts the matter with reference to his own practice, a replacement) of philosophy. Let's say this means that psychoanalysis is some specific continuation of the Platonic, Augustinian, Cartesian, Spinozistic, Kantian, Hegelian, Nietzschean legacy in the examination of the soul. This is a formulation that seems to me to capture my experience of the texts of Lacan that I have read, and to capture what I find attractive in them, but of course it is one that few American psychoanalysts or philosophers would be interested in or approve of, and yet I am indebted to them, too.

I took you to be asking me, in effect, what I mean by the name Lacan, and I am trying to respond uncontentiously. So perhaps I should simply declare that after reading Lacan's reading of, say, "On Narcissism" or *Beyond the Pleasure Principle* I find on returning to Freud's texts that Lacan's unpredicted remarks have not only taken me into them in new ways – one expects this of valuable reading – but that the conjunction of Lacan's texts with Freud's seems to have what I may call a therapeutic, liberating effect, and not only in my ability to read those texts. Is that a philosophical effect? Does it belong in a university? Reading Melanie Klein also produces such a therapeutic effect for me, but what she says seems on the surface so awkward and brusque that I usually cannot account for the source of her effect; it does not lie, so far as I can see in what I have read of her, in an illumination of Freud's language. Winnicott also has this effect, but his voice is so steady and impersonally engaging that I do not stop to ask how he does it.

It does not strike me as far-fetched to regard Lacan as having produced the most fruitful systematic reading there is of the Freudian corpus, one that allows it to challenge its readers and to challenge the idea of the sciences and the status of philosophy, in whose light it is written. But this leaves quite open the question of the value of reading, conserving, the Freudian text, as opposed to taking it as a collection of scientific papers and books, to be surpassed and replaced in other papers and books. So how shall we otherwise think of the relation of psychoanalysis and philosophy? Why, as Pierre Hadot, a major historian of ancient philosophy, has claimed, did philosophy for its first millennium, conceive of itself in relation to forms of spiritual excercise; or rather why, given that history, did this relation cease? Is this to be understood through the Heideggerean–Derridean perception of philosophy's break toward logocentrism?

**QUESTION**   I wonder if I could ask you one little thing more about this. And this might bring us back to Derrida again if you wish. My sense is that Lacanians are profoundly suspicious of Derrida. That there may be as great a hostility there, intellectual hostility perhaps, as there might be between ordinary language philosophers and

Derrida. I would be curious to know whether you sense that among Lacanians. Do you sense that there is something in Lacan that is, let us say, incompatible with the sort of thinking you see at work in Derrida's texts?

**CAVELL**   I doubt that I have anything helpful to say about this. I can see reasons for Lacanians to distrust Derrida. He is also a brilliant, if intermittent, reader of Freud, but one who is not going to subject himself to the Freudian text as Lacan does. You might say he wouldn't do this with any text, except that his relation to Heidegger, or Hegel, even in a more minor way his relation to Artaud or to Jabés or to Bataille, suggests a relation of something like introjection. Without them you would not have Derrida's prose, or he wouldn't have his margins. On the other hand, I'm not sure I know of a writer other than myself who finds Derrida to bear any such relation to ordinary language philosophy. If such a philosopher bothers, on the whole, to express hostility to Derrida, it is not likely to prompt an intellectual or detailed confrontation of his work. Whereas if a Lacanian does not succeed in ignoring Derrida, I do not see that the issue is settled as to which of them, if either, will be up for incorporation or rejection. I do not, I believe, know thinkers trying to find themselves who are deeply and equally engaged with both Derrida and Lacan.

When Austin speaks of and makes his appeal to the ordinary he does not, and neither does Wittgenstein, appeal to the squalor, the slips and chances, with which we encounter one another everyday. It is not a consultation of actual ordinary intercourse that they seek. I have styled their consultation an appeal to ordinary language against itself. Austin's and Wittgenstein's surprises of the everyday are not ones for which Derrida has much ear, or much patience. But who could be exempt from turning a deaf ear, sometimes, just here?

# The Self of Philosophy: An Interview with Stanley Cavell

The following interview with Richard Fleming took place on May 6, 1993.

**FLEMING** I would like to talk with you about your characterization of the history of philosophy. You sometimes present it as that which is in tension with the ordinary. In your comparisons between Austin and Derrida, for instance, you talk about the history of philosophy as a flight from the ordinary. However, another way you characterize it is discussed in your essay on Emerson titled "Finding as Founding." There your interest is in philosophy's historical desire to provide foundations yet (apparent) inability to establish them with the necessity or certainty sought. You go on to ask what it would mean if it couldn't do so, and where would philosophy find itself if it ceased to pursue foundations. I wonder if you would say some more about Emerson, finding as founding, and the history of philosophy.

**CAVELL** Well, let's see. Without trying to get too close in for the moment let me try to remember why it seemed to me so important to capture what Emerson meant. You are certainly right to catch the play there between the contingent and the necessary, or say between orientation and foundation. First let me talk about what I felt was

happening in Emerson and then about Emerson's relation
to the history of philosophy. I don't mean by this to dodge
the question about how I think finding and founding work
in the history of philosophy (if there is such a one thing as
a history of philosophy rather than a succession of responses that, as Thoreau pictures things in the third chapter of *Walden*, called "Reading," disperses the veils called,
among other things, history ("When that ancient Egyptian
or Hindoo philosopher first lifted the veil from the God-
dess, it was me in him. . . . And it is him in me now that
reviews the vision")). Whatever will be the founding of
philosophy will have something to do with where you find
yourself, in other words it will have something to do with
the discovery of what there is in the condition of the
human (at a juncture in history). If you find this a kind of
humanism in Emerson you should also find that it does
not go uncontested. There is, for instance, his claim to
know the world as not-me; and there is his involvement in
old ideas of God as in me – but is that a humanism or an
anti-humanism in Emerson? He casts these things into an
endless circulation. This is what my title "Finding as
Founding" is meant to mark. It is an idea at once of the
contingent in the necessary and the necessary in the contingent. I think of this as a methodological idea, but what
this comes to in Emerson is a way of seeing the work of his
writing; most specifically it points to a way of describing
the Emersonian sentence, often sensed as the key to
Emersonian thinking, sometimes to Emerson's credit,
sometimes not. I keep coming back to this, never sure that
I have done what I can to show the definiteness of the
concept of thinking in Emerson's hands – the writer most
often denied the title of philosopher by his readers.

Thinking, in "The American Scholar," Emerson's principal essay on thinking, is defined by two predicates, that
of conversion, or more precisely, aversion, and that of
transfiguration. Transfiguration here should in part be
seen as a term of rhetoric, one which speaks of the essen-

tial figurability of language, put this as the restlessness of what is said, or as it were, the inability to read a sentence every way it can be read in any one reading, or finding.

When Emerson proposes an image of a stairway in answer (in "Experience") to his opening question, Where do we find ourselves?, he is emphasizing that we do not know the difference between up and down, between, as Nietzsche puts the matter at the beginning of *Ecce Homo*, ascension and decadence, as fateful for the philosophical as for the religious aspiration. Images of stairways or ladders are ancient ones, from Jacob to Wittgenstein, and I am assuming that on Emerson's intermittent, contingent resting points of finding (to relate this specifically to the history of philosophy), something we might find on a given stair is the company of a philosopher. To find a philosopher at a step of American culture is for Emerson to found philosophy in America. I hope I am not slighting Jonathan Edwards, nor the English philosophers who are invoked by the founding fathers. I am assuming that the earlier American thinkers did not make an original philosophical contribution back to such philosophers as Locke, did not change his future history as he had changed theirs. Whether America has a philosophical contribution to make is, I take it, a persistent Emersonian question. It is one dimension of the great essay "Experience." There Emerson confronts not so much the history of philosophy as philosophy in various of its moments or manifestations or traditions.

**FLEMING**   The first of the traditions is what?

**CAVELL**   Plato is the earliest I have in mind. There are an endless set of preoccupations and reversals between Plato and Emerson, arising from what I call Emersonian Perfectionism, a dimension of the moral life for which Plato's *Republic* is a definitive instance. (This view is broached in my Carus Lectures, *Conditions Handsome and*

*Unhandsome.*) For one instance, we might take Emerson's stair as an allusion to climbing from Plato's Cave to Plato's Sun. I think it is worth pondering whether Plato's reliance on this directedness is not under criticism in "Self-Reliance," where Emerson announces that the moral life, or the taking on of one's self, requires risking that you cannot tell whether an intuition, or revelation, comes from above or from below.

**FLEMING**   You have indicated that sentiment when suggesting that you thought of the Cave itself as the ordinary.

**CAVELL**   Yes. Or as I might rather say, it is the first, or actual ordinary, as opposed to the transfigured, or eventual ordinary.

**FLEMING**   How is it that the Cave is the actual ordinary?

**CAVELL**   Well it is where you first encounter yourself. It is where the sense of irreality of your existence and the necessity for turning yourself around first presents itself. I am taking that as the origin of philosophy in the ordinary. The sense of irreality in "Experience" is specified as a loss of the direction in which reality is to be found, that it is not ahead.

I cannot invoke Emerson's "Experience," in a context in which a relation between generations of philosophers is in question, call this the question of the history of philosophy, without thinking of Nietzsche's answering (so I have claimed) the opening question of "Experience" ("Where do we find ourselves?") with the opening question of *The Genealogy of Morals* ("How should we have found ourselves since we have never sought ourselves?"). It is the relation to Nietzsche that for me has established the Emersonian text as a standpoint in philosophy before the rift of traditions that leads in one line to Wittgenstein, in another to Heidegger, which is to say, to a present of philosophy in which philosophy exists in two, shunning states, a present to which or from which I feel I can understand what I do to pertain. It is because Emerson is that kind of past present of philosophy, a point of relay (and if ever then always), that his incorporation of presents of the so-called history of philosophy (that is, of other intellectual events recognizeable as such relays) counts as continuing the history of philosophy, or just say, preserving philosophy (inheriting it by betraying it, handing it on by handing it over, out of hand). And if in Emerson's form, then in what form not? But what is Emerson's form?

Let me make a little clearer how intimate I find the connection between Emerson and Nietzsche to be. I mentioned Nietzsche's taking up Emerson on thinking as ascending and descending, as if joining or visiting higher and lower worlds. (Here, having mentioned Plato's Cave, I am invoking the end of *The Republic* in the Myth of Er.) Both, what is more, relate the issue to the continuities and discontinuities of the family. Emerson relates his writing of "Experience" – hence his writing as such – to his dead young son. Nietzsche relates the rises and falls of his life as a writer to his dead young father and his still living mother. In both there is the issue of what they bury in the body of their work and of what lasts in it. Emerson and Nietzsche – Nietzsche also burying Emerson in his body of work – are questioning the pertinence of any given individual's claim to an incorporation of philosophy, a claim to practice it, so preserve it (while, or by, escaping it, as it has been). Why it is that Emerson's decisive philosophical importance for Nietzsche evidently *cannot* be remembered by philosophers (hence by whom?) is a topic of separate and abiding interest for me.

**FLEMING**  This is possibly tangential, but it occurs to me that one of the passages in the foreword of *The Claim of*

*Reason* that bothers a lot of people is the one where you say I've been told I ought to read *On Certainty* but I'm not going to read it just because others press me to do it. I have to have a better, a more genuine, reason to do so. And people have said, But this will help you, this will help you understand what Wittgenstein is about. Nonetheless you resisted. Is your resisting tied to your sense of the history of philosophy and the philosophical moment needing to be genuine?

**CAVELL**   I like the idea. I have by now read *On Certainty* and I can see what people may have meant by saying that I should read it. (One friend copied out the passage for me in which Wittgenstein remarks that knowledge is based on acknowledgment.) I do not think it is as good or interesting a text as *Philosophical Investigations*, nor have I found it – though I may well be wrong – to contain ideas not in the *Investigations*. Now I suppose that nobody exactly claims that it is a better book, but I know that some people find it more congenial to read than the *Investigations* and read it and assign it in preference to the *Investigations*. It's the preference that I find suspicious. Put it this way: The text of Wittgenstein's that I have mostly responded to – felt I could understand in its responses to itself – has been the *Investigations*. How it relates to other texts of Wittgenstein is for me as open a question as how it relates to the texts of other writers. This speaks, I believe, to your perception of me as wanting to preserve the specificity of the philosophical moment, a perception I think is true. In that moment, following Thoreau, history as it were drops out, not, as for other philosophers, because the past is impertinent, but because it is no longer past.

This takes me back to our beginning in which I was to note several moments in which Emerson encounters earlier philosophy, encounters it philosophically, so I like to insist. The concept of experience in "Experience" may be seen as a crossroads of at least two major traditions or paths of philosophy. It invokes the empiricist concept of experience with its distinction between impressions and ideas – I mean that the terms "idea" and "impression" are hammered at in Emerson's prose, and transfigured. Then there is Kant's idea of experience as something formed by the synthesis of the manifold of appearances, initially under the forms of space and time. The Kantian idea is picked up and transfigured in Emerson's various plays with the ideas of succession, a key Kantian term in the establishing of the tradition of idealism, through the distinction between the succession of (inner) experiences and the succession of (outer) objects, hence his anchoring and mapping of a world of knowledge in functions of human understanding, and his consequent discovering of a world beyond this one, fixed in the aspiration of human reason. In Emerson's transfigurations, impression names not a uniform physical process but a mark of intellectual or spiritual achievement, an occurrence not to a tabula rasa, as something at the beginning, as it were, of the possession of a mind, but an occurrence to the rarely impressionable, causing as it were a flowering of mentality. Similarly, succession or success name not the process of assuring and reconstituting a given world but a step in a new (yet unapproachable, perhaps unfathomable) world.

In these various transfigurations, what happens to the philosophical idea of experience is that I no longer ask, "How can I use experience to relate myself to the world?" but rather "How can I recognize that I am not related to the world through the experience that I recognize in myself?" Emerson's answer to the strangeness of the world, his strangeness to it (estrangement is too weak an idea for this distance, suggesting that some known form of understanding might bring the parties back together), is that something has been lost to him permanently, figured by the death of his son, so that the idea of approaching the world comes through a kind of mourning for it.

**FLEMING**   I think you hit each moment you intended to discuss, but let me be sure you did. You started this by talking about several moments. They are?

**CAVELL**   What I had in mind was Plato, the Empiricists, and Kant. Elsewhere I have emphasized Descartes's presence in "Self-Reliance." But I get discouraged saying and repeating such things since the connections are of no interest to me in the absence of a recognition of the utter specificity of Emerson's taking on of the ideas. And I rarely feel I have taken sufficient time to make this unmistakable.

**FLEMING**   Let me now turn in a slightly different direction but still with a concern with Emerson. Specifically, let me ask about the response that some people have to you when you talk about Emerson. I've heard, on many occasions where you talk about Emerson, people gently (sometimes not so gently) trying to suggest that he can't be as important as you say or that his work while influencing Nietzsche cannot be as overriding as you suggest, or various things like that.

**CAVELL**   Right.

**FLEMING**   And I've heard you say and you have written that we all get around to condescending to Emerson. Now I thought about that and I said, well I think that's right. I think I do condescend to him. But what about your own case? Do you, in fact, find yourself finally either condescending or separating or wanting to draw away from Emerson, and where might that be?

**CAVELL**   I appreciate the question. I don't imagine that anyone can have thought less well of Emerson's pretenses to philosophy than I did, coming to him after my immersion in Thoreau's *Walden*. I found Emerson's sentences preposterous in their self-inflation and in the evident vagueness with which they treated philosophical ideas. So I was floored when its ideas started to dawn on me. There came a time, as with any text I feel I know, when every word seemed to have found its place. And then the judgment of imprecision and inaccuracy became so ludicrous that the judgment was turned against myself, and it was my resistance that came under scrutiny. Something of the sort had happened to me with Thoreau. I had found him drenched in cultural rumor – a nature writer of some well-recognized sort. America's ugly aggrandizing of itself together with its inability to appreciate its most elegant moments is painful sometimes to contemplate. Still, it has produced those moments, and some of them – like the appearances of Thoreau and of Emerson – help interpret the reactive aggrandizing, and so promise, for growing numbers of people I trust, to turn it to better purpose. At the present stage of my understanding, my discoveries of limitations in Emerson could not, I believe, present themselves to me as causes, or excuses, for condescension. Which means, I suppose, that I figure he knows as much about these limitations as I do. There are things I wish he would do better. I sometimes don't see in him enough concrete presence of the other for himself. As I sometimes don't see this in Thoreau, or forget how to recognize it. Then I hear someone rebuke Thoreau (the rebuke may once have been from me) for his solitude (rather as D'Alembert rebuked Rousseau for having shameful secrets that must be requiring such a craving for solitude – not seeing that such judgments are themselves causes for despair and flight), implying that it is easy to lead a utopian, even ecstatic, life if there are no other people around to spoil it; and it helps if someone lends you a nice site on a pond and someone else makes dinner for you in town.

Let us think about intellectual ingratitude, hardly less painful than other forms of ingratitude. Thoreau is preparing his place and inviting the presence of his other. He is writing, constructing his edification, for whoever comes

along, abiding, as for welcome, in his attractive spot in the
woods. So not to be there, reading him, is to resist him. To
describe him as alone is in effect to reject his company, to
annihilate it.

Are there no other Waldos in Emerson's life? He has in
any case said more than I know I have fathomed. If I leave
him – as he urges me to do, as Nietzsche imitates him (not
him alone) in urging me to do, aspiring to that kind of
founding, without being founders – I hope it will not be by
means of condescension (which would not really leave
him, and not intact, but would keep him bound to me, in
dissatisfaction).

**FLEMING**   I'm drawn to thinking about something you
say about Rousseau. Very late in *The Claim of Reason* you
talk about the *Confessions* and you talk about it as a text
written with a sense of creating another, creating another
who will care enough about the author to deal with the
difficulties of the book. I'm wondering if that's when you
might say one would be ungrateful not to accept such a
kind invitation. But to be so accepting of Rousseau or
Thoreau when he creates this environment is of course to
really have to modify myself. And I may have to be what I
don't want to be, sit with him in ways that should not be
demanded. I think this fits Emerson too. The reading of
him sentence by sentence or just taking a sentence and
letting it stand, this is not an easy thing to do. At least, it
is not easy for a lot of people, certainly not for me; it makes
Emerson difficult and a lifetime of work because of what it
takes to just spend the reflective time to recreate myself
with him. So I'm wondering if in your sense of a writer
welcoming an other, and others seeing what they are being
offered, I'm wondering not just if there are legitimate
grounds for condescension and a lack of gratitude, but if
there are not real grounds for personal concern, for destruction and loss of self?

**CAVELL**   So you do not find that Emerson lets go of you, even sends you on your way? I had hoped that that is what it means that, as I have put it, his work comes to an end in every sentence. It's what I mean when I say that *Walden* works to avoid suspense – why what he writes is not (and shows what it has against) fiction. But you are wanting here, perhaps, to think more about some of the paradoxes that some of these answers of mine skirt. You seem (partly) to want to ask: What is my freedom if I depend on another to find it for me?

**FLEMING**   That could be.

**CAVELL**   This paradox of finding freedom through the other is what Moral (or Emersonian) Perfectionism, as I understand it, sets out to try to articulate. We might for-mulate it as the question: Why does the Emersonian–Nietzschean idea of becoming what you are present itself as an injunction? Evidently the perception is that that is what being human is, what the relation of this mind to this body itself enjoins. (The double direction in the concept of enjoining – urging and prohibiting – is apt.) It lies in Emerson's sense of paradox in saying that freedom is fated. The paradox registers that freedom from others is a function of freedom from the other of yourself. (This is why, so I argue, Emerson's "Fate" has to bury in itself the horror of the institution of slavery.) My language is the language of others, or else it is not a language. But of which others? My world was mine to reject, and I rejected it before I knew it was mine. This is the problem about inheriting America. Emerson wishes to reject what was not his to accept, in a language unowned. There were others already here, always already. The paradox, in another reg-ister, extends to Freud's difficulties about primary and secondary narcissism: the other is the other as object of projection of myself; and yet it is other. The Socratic image of being called aside by one's genius records oneself mythically as other.

**FLEMING**   That leads me to the role the other plays in your own work. The deeper I read or the more I read your work, your texts, the more often I find words that are somebody else's. Now I don't know if you'd agree with that or not, but one does find in your work a lot of quotations, a lot of use of the words of others; sometimes without quotes you directly state what someone has said; and I think many people recognize this. But I'm wanting to suggest that as you continue from those places, where it seems most clearly to be you, where you are (maybe) taking a stand or staking a claim, I often find others there as well, populating every place, every phrase, every word. And I'm not surprised, but I'm wanting to know how you react to that kind of reading because there is a sense in which you're there and you're not there. (We're all there.) There is something representative yet there's something individual. I don't think I make that up.

**CAVELL**   No, no you don't. But I would like to be specific about this, and look at instances of the words or phrases of mine that you may have in mind. Quotation, conscious and unconscious, in homage or in envy, in health or in sickness, with acknowledgment or disparagement, free or fated, is an anxious subject, one Emerson devoted essential time to. I accept that you are talking exactly about what we were talking about a moment ago. What you reveal is a way I have of exploring the idea that the "having" of a self is being the other to one's self, calling upon it with the words of others. To find oneself on the plane of others is something my lecture on Emerson's "Fate" is critically about. It contains speculations about why it is that Emerson lays out his long lists of names, the figures on, or of, his mind. It is no wonder that in his America he craves intellectual company, and conjures it out of what sometimes seems thin air. How different is our America?

I keep coming back to aspects of the idea that the having of a language is an allegory of the having of a self. What does it mean for either a language or a self to be said to be mine? The question comes up in the Austin–Derrida material when I say that Austin is aware not just that I abandon my words to others but that I am abandoned to them, in them. That is a way I take Austin's picture of my hand's being tethered to my voice or breath (not exactly the way I put it in my lecture). I recognize words as mine when I see that I have to forgo them to use them. Pawn them and redeem them to own them. What does that say, otherwise (that is, allegorically), about having a self, that is about putting myself into the world, and receiving it from there? That having a self is, in Emerson's terms, abandoning it? In the first essay I wrote about Emerson I say that the task of the human being, contrary to Heidegger's discovery of it, is not to learn how to dwell but to learn how to leave, to learn abandonment (by whom? to what?) – and is that really contrary? Now suppose that this having by giving (or spending, as Thoreau sees it) is allegorized in every syllable that escapes you. Then the having of a self is allegorized in every syllable. The in and out of the breath is how Emerson, in "Fate," pictures thinking, the exchange of fate for freedom, the withstanding of the plenum of others. The breath is of course an ancient image of the soul or self. So what is happening, on my reading of "Fate," is that the self is – is identified as what is – breathed in and out.

Since I have never said just that before, I feel I have taken a step, and I'd like to stop here for the moment.

# Continuing Cavell: Side Roads of *The Claim of Reason*

If we accept as one of the principal claims of Stanley Cavell's *The Claim of Reason* that Ludwig Wittgenstein's *Philosophical Investigations* is endlessly in struggle with skepticism, then what does Cavell's writing teach us if not that we must finally live our skepticism, recognize the constant threat of madness that permeates our existence, replace metaphysical foundings of being with finding ourselves, embrace our finitude and ordinary existence rather than philosophically flee from them, and ask what our lives would look like if that work is realized? Once we have heard *The Claim of Reason's* confession that we must live the truth of skepticism how do we continue?

A reading of Cavell and certainly of *The Claim of Reason* uncovers a proposal that we stop our twenty-five-hundred-year fight with skepticism and live in the face of (which is not the same as living without) doubt. This would likely mean that an ambitious philosophy of our time might attempt to keep philosophy open to the threat of or temptation to skepticism rather than trying to refute it or give it a different and less destructive face. Cavell's Wittgenstein and writings can be read as having this ambition and pursuing its numerous demands. His is a philosophy that finds our everyday existence to be inhabited by skepticism, but not as something to be overcome, as if to be refuted, as if it is a conclusion about human knowledge (which is skepticism's preferred interpretation and traditional picture of itself), but as something to be placed as a mark of what Emerson calls the "human condition," so that skepticism's conversation and challenge are treated as a further interpretation of finitude, a mode of inhabiting our life, our stake, in words, in the world. Cavell's struggles in *The Claim of Reason* brought him to a definitive crossroad at which he concluded that philosophy's task was not so much to defeat the skeptical argument as to preserve it, as though the philosophical benefit of the argument would be to show not how it might end but why it must begin and why it must have no end, at least none within philosophy (can poetry's end be stated in poetry? is it not the place of others, of interdisciplinary study, to help with such concerns?). To live one's skepticism would not, therefore, for Cavell be simply to assert our natural condition as knowers (our non-knowing relationship to the world and others) but to suggest a way to inhabit that condition of doubt and thereby to situate or live our lives. Such a proposal allows us to wonder "what would happen to philosophy if it so viewed skepticism?" (What if we were to cease avoiding Cavell and acknowledge him instead?)

If one concedes that skepticism is a part of humanness and that absolute and certain foundations for our epistemological and moral claims will elude us, then where does the philosopher turn? Philosophical failures and disappointments force us back upon ourselves and turn us from the pursuit of empirical knowledge to the quest for self-knowledge. *The Claim of Reason* addresses this turn in its second paragraph, where Cavell "introduces himself" by insisting on understanding "philosophy not as a set of problems but as a set of texts." His insistence is necessary partly as a means of separating himself from recent analytical philosophy which largely views the discipline as aimed at problem solving. Cavell's writing in contrast does not employ arguments to produce theories to produce solutions to problems. His arguments do not aim to provide new theses or doctrines but seek rather to uncover the self that does such work in and with arguments. He transforms our sensibilities and redirects our interests (from the empirical to the self) with the claims of reason, the rights of skepticism. While some avoid Cavell and rest undisturbed at the prospect of philosophy forgoing its therapeutic, self-directed dimension, many others acknowledge him yet cannot rest easy at the idea of philosophy abandoning the business of argument. But suppose that what is meant by argumentation in philosophy is one way of accepting full responsibility for one's own discourse, confessing the reasons why one uses the words one does? This is Cavell's attention to argument, his means of reattaching our philosophical attention to what we say and mean. He does not abandon the philosophical concern with argument but does make us uneasy with ourselves, with our assured sense of what argument is, with what words are our own.

In a less sympathetic mood, the text rather than problem orientation of philosophy might be seen as a way of covering one's self-indulgences, one's personal whims, and the turn of philosophy to the subjective. Those with a marked concentration on self-knowledge can be charged with doing so under the cover or even with the goal of a narcissistic desire for self-expression rather than having the hard-fought-for Western aim of scientific wisdom and objective truth. This lack of sympathy and respect for the use and expression of oneself may, Cavell says, amount to "disbelieving that one could oneself contribute a philosophical text." It is as though Cavell wants us to understand those who pursue philosophy (wholly) in terms of (its) problems, as those who do so in the spirit of rejecting the value of the human subject as a source for philosophical expression or as the subject of proper philosophical investigation and pursuit. It is "as if to contribute a text were a kind of defacement." It is to make philosophy subjective and to make the problems of philosophy dependent on a personal self. Those who write and concentrate on texts do so, it can plausibly be charged, with the ego-centric goal of self-expression and self-knowledge. Rather than seeing such self-expression as a "defacement" of the discipline, Cavell sees self-knowledge as the proper sub-ject-matter and pursuit of the philosopher.

This turn to and quest for self-knowledge can be found in each part of *The Claim of Reason* and in the text as a whole. Philosophy as Cavell in this text tries to understand it and pursue it must push beyond saying something is true or false, or merely grasping the argument, problem, or conclusion uttered. It must consider the finite (human) being who says what is true or false. Why and for what reason does someone give such and such an argument?

Certainly analytical philosophy cannot be charged with completely ignoring or disagreeing with this; even the most common mode of presentation of analytical philoso-phy shows this interest. The form of writing that is the body and soul of analytical philosophy is the academic paper and it is intentionally "modest in its aim, content with its minor addition to a subject greater than itself" and this is the way problems and text, objective truths and subjective self get combined. Cavell does not contest the "comparative greatness of the subject over the subjects" but "would be more convinced of academic modesty" if he had not so often been confronted by those who "are daily surprised that, for example, Descartes or Pascal or Rousseau, or the spirit of religion or of rationalism or of romanticism, has survived the criticism fashioned in their essay on the subject a few years back." To this report on the state of philosophy he adds, "I speak of professional lives, frightening matters." This is a critical condemnation not of the genre of the philosophical article itself, but of the way it is used by those who concentrate on problems rather than texts, a strong criticism of the spirit in which analytical philosophers talk and work. (Such indirect criti-cism is paradigmatic of Cavell's critical writing about

others. He often willingly grants the expertise and sincerity of another (the reasonableness of their concerns) but
questions the spirit and use (usually the narrowness of the
spirit and use) given the content written (spoken). He
attempts to show us that our words often do not mean
what we say, that we easily lose control of them. Our loss
of control is not necessarily over what words mean but
what we mean in using them when and where we do. We
easily lose a sense of ourselves and of the context of
language use in which we speak.)

At an early stage in his writing (*The Senses of Walden*),
Cavell asks, "Why has America never expressed itself
philosophically? Or has it . . . ?" The context of the questions implies that he was taking the question of American
philosophical expression to be linked with the question
whether Thoreau and Emerson are to be recognized as
philosophers. But what can he be asking here? It isn't as if
he did not know in the early 1970s that philosophy in the
United States had assumed the leadership of what is called
Anglo-American analytical philosophy, which is half of
what the Western world calls philosophy. Or that he was
unaware that pragmatism was (is) often cited as the unique
American contribution to world philosophy. Given that he
knew such things, what could Cavell have been and still be
asking about American philosophy? As we continue to
read and struggle with Cavell's writings we come to see
that he wanted and wants us to wonder whether American
analytical philosophy or American pragmatism are expressive of American thought in the way thought can be or has
been expressed. Can we even reasonably ask such a question about the expressions of thought? How does, how has,
philosophy expressed itself? Cavell would like his questions about problems and texts to help us discover what
can genuinely and reasonably be asked about (American)
philosophy, and its forms of self-expression.

But hasn't Cavell in so presenting his wishes about texts
actually sided (perhaps unwittingly) with the analytical

camp and betrayed his own intentions? Isn't the claim about the importance of texts over problems itself a philosophical problem that must be solved, viz., what is a philosophical text? Certainly his claim is not a text, is it? Cavell's writing is meant to raise questions about what philosophical thought and writing are, and we are immersed in these questions immediately in (the second paragraph of) *The Claim of Reason.* The length or number of words, says Cavell, does not decide what is a problem or what is a text. The shortness of the story of the Cretan Truth-teller or of the one about the tree falling in a forest does not keep them from being texts. Similarly there are long books such as Hume's *Treatise* that have been treated as though they were a set of problems. Some texts like Descartes's *Meditations* are short books whose methods of reaching disreputable conclusions come to be the problem of concern. Other texts are "for practical purposes as unending as the writing of, for example, Kant or Hegel, where the problem resides largely in mastering the text itself." In such texts one must resign oneself to commentary and to being marginal or working in the margins of another's text, using words that are not one's own.

In sharpening our concern for a diagnosis of philosophical motivation, we must ask ourselves not whether Cavell has unwittingly sided with analytical philosophy by giving us a new problem (whether philosophy is texts or problems) but rather ask in what spirit he presents his insistence that we see philosophy as texts rather than problems. As mentioned, Cavell's insistence is a means of separating himself from analytical philosophy, and part of its spirit is one of distancing himself from and solidifying his position in opposition to the spirit of analytical philosophy. But Cavell so hardens his position, as a continuing reading shows, not because he has a lack of regard for analytical philosophy, or because he sees his work as an alternative to analytical philosophy (which were perspectives given to many by his pre-*The Claim of Reason* writings), but because he no longer wishes to be seen and read as fighting with or being in competition with the context of analytical philosophy. Such a battle is not the point of his work, and he is too far removed from its spirit to be in conflict with it. Hence the phrases "separating himself from . . ." and "distancing himself from . . . analytical philosophy" are not quite right. They are too much like asking "can ought be derived from is?" or "can you go from Canada to Toronto?" There just is no separation or distance of the expected kind between them. By removing himself from the problem-solving view of philosophy, Cavell hopes to make us ask the question about both analytical philosophy and his own work: in what spirit are they done?

Philosophy must not forget or avoid the finite human being who stands at the center of philosophical expression. To understand this is to understand why Cavell begins his discussion of texts and problems by "introducing himself." His introduction is a reminder that he stands behind these sentences we are reading and that his being is that on which *The Claim of Reason* is based. Analytical philosophers who find such introductions irrelevant and who see philosophy as problems to be solved will not only be forgetting the human context that allows their inquiry to proceed meaningfully, but will also be lacking a context in which to understand the limits of their own interests and being; problems removed from human context have no restricting criteria, and hence no limits that can establish their correct or incorrect use. (As an aside to this path of thought it might be worth noting, for those who have the tolerance for such self-reflection, that if – as Christopher Norris and even Derrida have suggested – a proper understanding of the spirit of the work of deconstruction involves seeing it as the "rigorous consequence, not only of structuralist thinking but of any linguistic philosophy basing its methods on the principle that meaning determines [or precedes] reference," if, that is, Derrida has general ties to standard analytical philosophy – even if the resulting aims be different – then the concerns voiced above about analytical philosophy may embrace deconstructive writing. Too often deconstructive procedures, not unlike analytical procedures, seem to wish to bring philosophy a false peace, which may well present itself in the form of bustling activity. The two, as flights from the ordinary, might stand or fall together and the worthy or significant other they both must confront is Stanley Cavell – which is to say Wittgenstein.)

The importance of self-knowledge and self-expression as a proper pursuit for the discipline of philosophy and as a means of understanding Continental and analytical philosophical concerns has its dominant place in *The Claim of Reason* but (like many investigations) Cavell's perspective can be opened and his voice in philosophy clarified and reanimated if we take a wider look around, if we read beyond *The Claim of Reason*.

Certainly Cavell's reading of Emerson can provide this wider perspective. Emerson represents the important change toward skepticism which philosophy is challenged by Cavell to accept. In his first writings ("Nature") Emerson takes skepticism to be refutable and solvable but in his later work ("Experience") he comes to find it unsolvable and at the heart of his thinking and our being. Can philosophy so change itself? What kind of suggestion is this? An ongoing reading of Cavell's writings helps answer such questions as it elicits his wondering what would happen to philosophy if we took the search for foundations from it and replaced it with the search for finding oneself? There is nothing overly unique or remarkable about this possibility, at least nothing that cannot be found in aspects of ordinary language philosophy (as it is represented to some extent in Austin and especially in Wittgenstein), as the latter is interpreted by Cavell. Cavell sees Emerson (and Thoreau) as foreshadowing the work done in ordinary language philosophy, in the attention each gives to the familiar, the everyday, the common. This means that

Cavell sees both American transcendentalism and ordinary language philosophy as responses to anxiety about
our human capacities as knowers, as responses to our
human subjection to doubt. The emphasis finally is not on
the ordinariness of what is said but on the fact that it is
said or written by human beings, in a language they share.
Ordinary language philosophy, along with Emerson and
Thoreau, wishes "to put the human animal back into
language and therewith back into philosophy." To live my
skepticism, to recover from skepticism is to recover from
the drive to the inhuman, to recover the self, to recover
and find my ordinary, human voice.

If whatever will be the founding of philosophy will have
something to do with where you find yourself then what do
we understand Cavell to be doing? What do we understand
Cavell doing after we have understood his confession that
we must live the truth of skepticism? One answer is that
by replacing founding with finding we get Wittgenstein
and that (American) philosophy that underwrites
Wittgenstein's devotion to the ordinary – Emerson and
Thoreau. If we accept Cavell's reading of Wittgenstein
(if we accept Emerson and Thoreau as philosophers)
we explode philosophy from the inside. We destroy (European) philosophy or philosophy as a present (European)
phenomenon. (American philosophy is not European
philosophy.)

While Cavell sees himself, when making such sugges-
tions, engaged in instruction through provocation, nothing
less than trauma can accompany the freedom that comes
with such thoughts, and a loss of one's history seems most
probable. The question of the place and worth of philosophy is open in Cavell much in the same way it is open in
Emerson. When American philosophers challenge the
state of European philosophy, are we to understand philosophy as a treasure to be won for America from Europe,
or is it to be regarded as the great European construction
of thought, which American thinking is to overcome, or is

there an American philosophical difference to be contributed in philosophy's further construction? Cavell's work keeps the question open as to where philosophy occurs and what it looks like. Cavell is an American philosopher who wishes to place his skepticism, and who writes to provoke Emersonian concerns with the state of philosophy, and (more generally) attempts to provide us with his particular American incentive for thinking about philosophy, through examining and uncovering the conditions for thinking, living his thinking, attracting us to (Emersonian) thinking as a partial act or to its partiality. In such a way we can understand Cavell's preference to "leave everything" he says or has said "as in a sense provisional," meaning "that it is to be gone on from." If that going on is to the further derivation of his ideas, which philosophers seem to crave, so much the better, but if not, that only means philosophy should question and distrust its own defenses of what it is, and its historical recreations of itself.

To the extent that Cavell accepts that philosophy has a history and can be said to progress, he often prefers to see that history and progress as one of displacement. Philosophers displace, put in a new place, one particular idea for another with the new idea related to the original by discernable associations. In a general sense the foundational epistemology of the Moderns can be read as placing only to displace the Being of the Ancients, not unlike the way the concerns with language in contemporary philosophy put the epistemology and metaphysics of the Moderns and Ancients in their place. The process of displacement in the work of philosophy does, however, have an even more Freudian meaning, and for Cavell a more important sense in the discipline, than simply the favoring of one idea over another. The attempt to displace a particular philosophical idea of ground or foundation, a displacement which constitutes the scene or the work of philosophical progress in the revelation of new, unquestionable grounds, is, claims Cavell, best understood as revealing the importance of a quest for the ordinary. In the search for unshakeable grounds and absolute foundations the avoidance of the ordinary – the ordinary being antithetical to metaphysical or epistemological or any kind of inhuman certitude – is disclosed and hence the importance of the latter. Instead of confronting our everyday selves and world we substitute for it, exchange for it, the search for empirical knowledge (regardless of whether we finally believe in the success of, or in the need to supplement, such knowledge). The pursuit of self-knowledge (the quest to know ourselves) is displaced by a search for Being and Knowledge independent of the self. Furthermore, the very characterization of philosophy as something having a history and a line or lawful and rational path is a deviation of thought, a substitution of founding for finding. It is to give an importance to the history of philosophy, to the being and objectivity of history, rather than to the confrontation and pursuit of oneself. In this sense, traditional, Western philosophy, its history, can be characterized, and is often so characterized by Cavell, as a flight from the ordinary. Until we are ready to replace (metaphysical) foundings of being with finding ourselves – or (better) accept the dialectical tension between them – it will so remain.

Such an understanding of philosophy can be heard in Wittgenstein's declaration that the task (his task) of philosophy is the bringing of our words back (from their metaphysical) to (everyday) life. (Wittgenstein may accordingly be labeled a philosopher of metaphysical language as accurately as a philosopher of ordinary language. Neither one is accurate without the other.) In so saying he discerns and wishes to distinguish two kinds of philosophical work. In one we imitatively (listening to our history) declare our uniqueness (the theme of skepticism); in the other, we originally (ordinarily) declare our commonness (the theme of acknowledgment).

The way the words of our elders, the way the history of philosophy, (can) chagrin us, the way we imitatively declare our uniqueness challenges our identity of ourselves and reveals another central concern of Cavell's work. When our elders, their words, embarrass us, leave us flat, what choices do we have? Find other elders? Find our own (new) words? These questions reanimate philosophical concerns with self-expression and texts, and touch on a duality found in the discipline's earliest days, "the division between Plato's writing and Socrates' talking." Such a concern with texts and history is purely "illustrated in this century by contrasting Heidegger's work, which assumes the march of the great names in the whole history of Western philosophy, with that of Wittgenstein, who may get around to mentioning half a dozen names, but then only to identify a remark which he happens to have come across and which seems to get its philosophical importance only from the fact that he finds himself thinking about it". Common to these two myths of reading is an idea "that philosophy begins only when there are no further texts to read, when the truth you seek has already been missed, as if it lies behind you. In the myth of totality, philosophy has still not found itself – until at least it has found you; in the myth of emptiness, philosophy has lost itself in its first utterances". In a similar vein, Emerson writes, "Man dares not say . . . but quotes," and by so suggesting that saying is quoting he condenses a number of ideas. First, that language is an inheritance. Words are before I am; they are common. Second, the question whether I am saying them or quoting them, saying them firsthand or secondhand, means to ask whether I am thinking or imitating, which is the same as the question whether I do or do not exist as a unique human being and is a matter demanding proof. Third, the writing of words not my own while stressing a concern with one's existence and the inheritance of language, an owning of words, does not remove words from circulation but rather returns them to life, brings them back from their metaphysical (disowned state) to their everyday use. The claim to existence requires returning words to language as if making them common to us.

Continuing on this side road, the idea that with every word you utter you say more than you know you say means in part that you do not know in the moment the extent to which your saying is quoting. As one reads more and more deeply (continuously) in Cavell's writings one gains a sense that all his words are someone else's. This experience strikes one even on first readings. Numerous passages are quoted and works referred to without footnote or specific reference. (Doesn't such a use of others show the impoverished state of his thinking? Isn't Cavell's work intellectually and creatively weak because of its inherent reliance on voices and texts not his own? On the contrary, it reaffirms his connections with others; it shows the deep trust Cavell has in others and in himself; it exemplifies the belief that what is true for you, in your "private" experience, is true for all humans.) The more (deeply) we read into Cavell the more we find not Cavell but a multitude of others. We find all the others, the many voices, that make Cavell what he is and that he carries with him wherever he goes. This is possibly a way of saying what *The Claim of Reason* has already said to us: pursuit of the self reveals the other. We finally (must) find ourselves in others. The soul is impersonal. No matter how far we go in investigations of the self we do not find anything special to us. (We discover that we can (must) search within ourselves for understanding and remedies to the human condition.) Hence a problem encountered in continuing to read and search for Cavell is that the text's thoughts and voices are neither exactly Cavell's nor not Cavell's. In their state of, say, repressed thoughts, they represent his further, next, unattained but attainable, self. To think otherwise, is to attribute the origin of his thoughts simply to the other, thoughts which are then, as it were, implanted in him by let us say some Wittgenstein or Emerson or Thoreau, which is to lose the self, lose Cavell, not acknowledge the confession he is making. The *Philosophical Investigations* (or a reading of *The*

*Claim of Reason*) discovers, for the discipline of philosophy, the problem of the other, and the finding or losing of
oneself in another is a way not to transcend history but for
time and place to fall away as if history had never (or had
not yet) begun; without acknowledgment there can be no
beginning.

All my words are someone else's. What but philosophy,
of a certain kind, would tolerate the thought?

## Appendix: The Source Text for "Continuing Cavell"

[What I call the "source text," and print here as an appen-
dix to my own text on Cavell, is the basis on which my text
was written. The source text consists of my selection and
ordering of sentences taken from texts produced by
Cavell, specifically from the following: *Conditions Handsome and Unhandsome*, University of Chicago Press, 1990;
*This New Yet Unapproachable America*, Living Batch Press,
1989; *In Quest of the Ordinary*, University of Chicago
Press, 1988; *The Claim of Reason*, Oxford University Press,
1979; and Cavell's responses in the two interviews in *The
Senses of Stanley Cavell* and the interview [and seminar] in
the present volume. One reason for my so writing about
Cavell is that I find reading him to be both an act of
discovery (finding things you had not seen, known, or
found before) and a stimulus for self-investigation and
personal pursuits (provocation to remove oneself from his
positions and stake one's own claims; wondering how one
does and can express oneself). Continuing (to read)
Cavell reveals both of these strands of philosophy and
should I believe push one back to his texts and forward to
finding oneself.]

What happens to philosophy if its claim to provide
foundations is removed from it – say the founding of
morality in reason or in passion, of society in contract, of
science in transcendental logic, of ideas in impressions,
of language in universals or in a formalism of rules? (The

idea of foundation as getting to the bottom once and for all of all things is a picture Thoreau jokes about in describing in "The Pond in Winter" and "Conclusion" in *Walden*, the time he took measurements of the bottom of Walden, and times such measurements become controversial.) The step I am taking here is to receive the work of "Experience" as transforming or replacing founding with finding and to ask what our lives would look like if the work is realized. I realize, as elsewhere, that speculation about matters such as these will offend certain philosophical sensibilities. If we accept Emerson as philosopher we explode philosophy from the inside . . . the question is open in Emerson as to whether in challenging philosophy we are to understand philosophy as a prize to be won for America from Europe, or whether we are to regard philosophy as the great European construction of thought, which, as such, our thinking is to overcome, or whether there is an American philosophical difference to be contributed in philosophy's further construction; and hence that the question is kept open as to where philosophy occurs, what it looks like, at which gate it sits, in the intellectual economy of a nation. This is worth saying if it encourages us to consider that Emerson's word "ground" in "Here are materials strewn along the ground" is to be given the weight of, or the place of, or the power to displace, the philosophical idea of ground or foundation, a displacement which constitutes the scene or the work of philosophical progress in the essay "Experience," where the progress of philosophy is called "success," not in irony but in transfiguring earnestness. Finding ourselves on a certain step we may feel the loss of foundation to be traumatic, to mean the ground of the world falling away, the bottom of things dropping out, ourselves foundered, sunk on a stair. But on another step we may feel this idea of (lack of) foundation to be impertinent, an old thought for an old world. As if he anticipates that a reader might suppose him accordingly to be opposed to the Enlightenment, he will famously also say, "I ask not for the great, the remote, the romantic; . . . I embrace the common, I sit at the feet of the familiar, the low," a claim I have taken as underwriting ordinary language philosophy's devotion to the ordinary, surely one inheritance of the Enlightenment. A fact to be impressed by in Wittgenstein and Austin is their use and devotion to the use of examples, stories, concrete matters. In them the emphasis is less on the ordinariness of an expression (which seems mostly to mean, from Moore to Austin, an expression not used solely by philosophers) than on the fact that they are said (or, of course, written) by human beings, in definite contexts, in a language they share . . . to put the human animal back into language and therewith back into philosophy . . . their attention to the language of ordinary or everyday life, is underwritten by Emerson and Thoreau in their devotion to the thing they call the common, the familiar, the near, the low. The connection means that I see both developments – ordinary language philosophy and American transcendentalism – as responses to skepticism, to that anxiety about our human capacities as knowers that can be taken to open modern philosophy in Descartes, interpreted by that philosophy as our human subjection to doubt. Suppose that Descartes discovered for philosophy that to confront the threat of, or temptation to, skepticism is to risk madness. Then since according to me the *Investigations* at every point confronts this temptation and finds its victory exactly in never claiming a final philosophical victory over (the temptation to) skepticism, which would mean a victory over the human, its philosopher has to learn to place and to replace madness, to deny nothing, at every point. Nevertheless I think it is true that the Wittgensteinian fervor is peculiarly vulnerable to a charlatanry (there are others) that philosophy should of all disciplines want most perfectly to free itself from. So it is worth considering that the sense of Wittgenstein's uniqueness, which I share, comes from the sense that he is joining the fate of philosophy as such with that of the philosophy or criticism of culture, thus displacing both – endlessly forgoing, rebuking, parodying philosophy's claim to a privileged perspective on its culture, call it the perspective of reason (perhaps shared with science); anyway forgoing for philosophy any claim to perspective that goes beyond its perspective on itself. And when Wittgenstein finds the task of philosophy to be the bringing of our words back to (everyday) life, he in effect discerns two grades of quotation, imitation, repetition. In one we imitatively declare our uniqueness (the theme of skepticism); in the other, we originally declare our commonness (the theme of acknowledgment). In Wittgenstein's *Philosophical Investigations* the issue of the everyday is the issue of the siting of skepticism, not as something to be overcome, as if to be refuted, as if it is a conclusion about human knowledge (which is skepticism's self-interpretation), but to be placed as a mark of what Emerson calls "human condition," a further interpretation of finitude, a mode, as said, of inhabiting our investment in words, in the world. A Wittgensteinian example gives us no prior path; it leaves no footprints . . . even when the acceptance of Wittgenstein as one of the major philosophical voices in the West since Kant may be taken for granted, it is apt to be controversial to find that his reception by professional philosophy is insufficient, that the spiritual fervor or seriousness of his writing is internal to his teaching, say the manner (or method) to the substance, and that something in the very professionalization of philosophy debars professional philosophers from taking his seriousness seriously. The feature I am trying to place intuitively within the overlapping of the regions of Kant and Emerson and Wittgenstein lies, I might say, not in their deflections of skepticism but in their respect for it, as for a worthy other; I think of it as their recognition not of the uncertainty or failure of our knowledge but of our disappointment with its success. I would characterize the difference by saying that in "Nature" Emerson is taking the issue of skepticism as solvable or controllable whereas thereafter he takes its unsolvability to the heart of his

thinking. Since a principal claim of *The Claim of Reason* is
that Wittgenstein's *Investigations* is endlessly in struggle
with skepticism, my various interpretations of skepticism
can be taken as indications of how what Wittgenstein calls
"ideal conditions in a sense," this frozen emptiness of
sublimity, is in turn to be interpreted. . . . I came to the
idea that philosophy's task was not so much to defeat the
skeptical argument as to preserve it, as though the philosophical profit of the argument would be to show not how
it might end but why it must begin and why it must have
no end, at least none within philosophy, or what we think
of as philosophy. Let us speak of a recovery from skepticism. This means, as said, from a drive to the inhuman.
Then why does this present itself as a recovery of the self?
Why, more particularly, as the recovery of the (of my)
(ordinary) (human) voice? But in all philosophical seriousness, a recovery from what? I wanted to answer by saying
that by the end of the first two parts of that book I had
convinced myself not only that there is no such solution,
that to think otherwise is skepticism's own self-in-tempta-
tion, but that it seemed to me, on the contrary, work for an
ambitious philosophy to attempt to keep philosophy open
to the threat or temptation to skepticism. Now I will say:
I live my skepticism. One is responsible for finding the
journey's end in every step of the road, in one's own gait.
When one mind finds itself or loses itself in another, time
and place seem to fall away – not as if history is tran-
scended but as if it has not begun. To live in the face of
doubt . . . the idea of communicating as emitting a breath
every moment . . . means that with every word you utter
you say more than you know you say . . . which means in
part that you do not know in the moment the extent to
which your saying is quoting. When Emerson notices, in
"Self-Reliance," that "every word they say chagrins us," he
is responding to the sound of quotation, imitation, repetition (conformity, confinement, etc.), but for him this
sound sets a task of practice, not (merely) a routine for

metaphysics – rather, it criticizes metaphysics not as a necessary defeat of thought but as a historical defeat of practice. Since the lives of this people, Emerson's people, do not yet contain thinking, he cannot, or will not, sharing this life, quite claim to be thinking. But he makes a prior claim, the enormous one I just alluded to, namely to be providing this incentive of thinking, laying the conditions for thinking, becoming its "source," calling for it, attracting it to its partiality, by what he calls living his thoughts, which is pertinent to us so far as his writing is this life; which means, so far as "the grandeur of justice shine(s)" in the writing and "affection cheer(s)" it. Think of it this way: if the thoughts of a text such as Emerson's (say the brief text on rejected thoughts) are yours, then you do not need them. If the thoughts are not yours, they will not do you good. The problem is that the text's thoughts are neither exactly mine nor not mine. In their sublimity as my rejected – say repressed – thoughts, they represent my further, next, unattained but attainable, self. To think otherwise, is to attribute the origin of my thoughts simply to the other, thoughts which are then, as it were, implanted in me – some would say caused – by let us say some Emerson, is idolatry. Emerson writes, "Man dares not say . . . but quotes." Emerson's gag, suggesting that saying is quoting, condenses a number of ideas. First language is an inheritance. Words are before I am; they are common. Second, the question whether I am saying them or quoting them – saying them firsthand or secondhand, as it were which means whether I am thinking or imitating, is the same as the question whether I do or do not exist as a human being and is a matter demanding proof. Third, the writing, of which the gag is part, is an expression of the proof of saying "I," hence of the claim that writing is a matter, say the decision, of life and death, and that what this comes to is the inheritance of language, an owning of words, which does not remove them from circulation but rather returns them, as to life. That the claim to existence requires returning words to language as if making them common to us, is suggested by the fourth sentence of "Self-Reliance": "To believe your own thought, to believe that what is true for you in your private heart is true for all men, – that is genius." About my own sound it may help to say that while I may often leave ideas in what seems a more literary state, sometimes in a more psychoanalytic state, than a philosopher might wish – that is, that a philosopher might prefer a further philosophical derivation of the ideas – I mean to leave everything I will say, or have, I guess, ever said, as in a sense provisional, the sense that it is to be gone on from. If a further derivation in philosophical form, so much the better; but I would not lose the intuitions in the meantime – among them the intuition that philosophy should sometimes distrust its defenses of philosophical form. And while someone may rest undisturbed at the prospect of philosophy forgoing its therapeutic dimension, no one should rest easy at the idea of philosophy abandoning the business of argument. But suppose that what is meant by argumentation in philosophy is one way of accepting full responsibility for one's own discourse. At one point in writing *The Senses of Walden*, I found myself asking, "Why has America never expressed itself philosophically? Or has it . . . ?" And the context of the question implied that I was taking the question of American philosophical expression to be tied up with the question whether Thoreau (and Emerson) are to be recognized as philosophers. It isn't as if I did not know in 1970 that America was pretty well assuming the leadership of what is called Anglo-American analytical philosophy, which is half of what the Western world calls philosophy. It was and is just as much a question for me whether pragmatism, often cited as the American contribution to world philosophy, was expressive of American thought – in the way I felt that thought could be or had been expressed. Is this a reasonable question? . . . I have wished to understand philosophy not as a set of problems but as a set of texts. This means to me that the contribution of a philosopher – anyway of a creative thinker – to the subject of philosophy is not to be understood as a contribution to, or of, a set of given problems, although both historians and non-historians of the subject are given to suppose otherwise. Some philosophical texts are for practical purposes as unending as the writings of, for example, Kant or Hegel, where the problem resides largely in mastering the text itself, hence in commentary; as though if one could believe all of it there would from then on be no isolating problems of belief left. Here contribution consists in opting to be marginal (which is of course not the only way of being marginal). Too often deconstructive procedures (like analytical procedures) seem to me readily used to bring philosophy a false peace, which may well present itself in the form of bustling activity. I speak of professional lives, frightening matters. Does the profession of philosophy have a history or is it a series of displacements? In the one myth the philosopher proceeds from having read everything, in the other from having read nothing. Perhaps this duality is prefigured in the division between Plato's writing and Socrates' talking, but it is purely illustrated in this century by contrasting Heidegger's work, which assumes the march of the great names in the whole history of Western philosophy, with that of Wittgenstein, who may get around to mentioning half-a-dozen names, but then only to identify a remark which he happens to have come across and which seems to get its philosophical importance only from the fact that he finds himself thinking about it. Common to the two myths is an idea that philosophy begins only when there are no further texts to read, when the truth you seek has already been missed, as if it lies behind you. In the myth of totality, philosophy has still not found itself – until at least it has found you; in the myth of emptiness, philosophy has lost itself in its first utterances. All my words are someone else's. What but philosophy, of a certain kind, would tolerate the thought?

Richard Fleming

# Notes and Afterthoughts on the Opening of Wittgenstein's *Investigations*

The notes to follow formed the basis of the first weeks of a lecture course on *Philosophical Investigations* initially given at Berkeley in 1960, then irregularly at Harvard and progressively amplified some half dozen times through the 1960s and 1970s. The last such set of lectures, offered in 1984, was radically altered since by then my *Claim of Reason* had appeared. I would not have thought to present these notes without entering into a sort of uneven, late conversation with them, preceding, interrupting, and succeeding them with certain afterthoughts a decade after they were used in a classroom. Why this presentation was made in 1991, and to what purpose, will emerge. The lecture notes appear in italic type, the afterthoughts in upright. Of course – it is more or less the point of the enterprise – I begin with afterthoughts.

The clearest unchanging feature of the course over the decades was the opening question: How does the *Investigations* begin? Against even the brief, varying introductory remarks I would provide – all omitted here – concerning Wittgenstein's life and his place in twentieth-century philosophy, in which I emphasized the remarkable look and sound of Wittgenstein's text and related this to issues of modernism in the major arts, the opening question was meant to invoke the questions: How does philosophy begin? And how does the *Investigations* account for its beginning (hence philosophy's) as it does? And since this is supposed to be a work of philosophy (but how do we tell this?), how does it (and must it? but can it?) account for its look and sound?

A number of reasons move me to make the notes public.

1    There is still, I believe, no canonical way of teaching the *Investigations* (unless beginning with the *Tractatus* and contrasting the *Investigations* with it counts as such a way), and young teachers have expressed to me their greatest dissatisfaction with their own teaching of it precisely over the opening weeks; typically, it seems to me, because they are unsure that when they step back from Wittgenstein's text they are doing justice to their sense of the particularity of that text. (To give some account of what has been called its "fervor," sensed as something like its moral drive, is among the motives of my "Declining Decline," in *This New Yet Unapproachable America*.) Some who attended my lectures, and others who know of them, have suggested that their publication might accordingly be of pedagogical help.

2    I had thought that these lectures would provide a beginning for what became *The Claim of Reason*, but I did not manage in preparing a final version of that manuscript to get them to motivate its present opening – with its focus on criteria, leading straight to the issue of the role of skepticism in the *Investigations* – well enough to justify their significant lengthening of an already lengthy book. I think I may be able to do better this time around. What's left of these opening lectures in *The Claim of Reason*, or epitomized there, is its paragraph-length opening sentence.

3    Because these lectures began as I was publishing my first two papers (the first two of what became *Must We Mean What We Say?*); and, as will emerge here, because the subject of beginnings is immediately on my mind as

I have turned to work on certain autobiographical materials; and because the precipitating stimulus for making these notes presentable was to distribute them to the members of the seminar I offered at the School of Criticism and Theory at Dartmouth in the summer of 1991, where the members varied in culture, in field, and in age, so that the common thread through the range of work I asked them to think about was the fact of its running through the work I do; I allowed myself, as these notes proceeded, to locate various crossroads as they come in view in the intellectual geography implied by texts I had published, or was preparing to publish, sometimes quoting bits of them when they seemed to me both clarifying and to exist in a fuller, or stranger, or more familiar, context that one or another reader might one or another day wish to explore.

4   There is an independent reason for wanting a readable statement of this material. Whatever its shortcomings in placing the opening of *The Claim of Reason*, it will help me place a recent turn in my thinking about the state of the child "learning" language, as presented in Augustine's portrait of (that is, his literary–philosophical remembering of himself as) such a child, which Wittgenstein uses to open his own book (his "album," he calls it) of literary–philosophical reminders. This recent turn, which was a significant feature of the greatly modified 1984 lectures, is sketched at the end of my consideration (in chapter 2 of *Conditions Handsome and Unhandsome*) of Kripke's *Wittgenstein on Rules and Private Language*. This will come up in good time, when its possible value can be more readily assessed.

Since preserving the individual strata of the versions from 1960 to 1979 is of no interest to me here, and since the process of revision was a normal part of preparing successive versions, I mostly assume that the later are the better ones and mostly just give those. I have made a conscious effort to leave the wording of the notes (except for filling in their telegraphese) as it is. When I was moved to intervene in the moment of transcription (mostly the spring of 1991), this is indicated, if the fact is not sufficiently obvious from the context, by reverting from italic to regular type.

I

*How does* Philosophical Investigations *begin? There are many answers, or directions of answer.*

*One might say, uncontroversially: It begins with some words of someone else. But why say this? Perhaps to suggest that Wittgenstein (but what or who Wittgenstein is is, of course, not determined), is not led to philosophical reflection from his own voice (or what might be recognized, right off, as his own voice), but from, as it were, being* accosted. *The accosting is by someone Wittgenstein cares about and has to take seriously; in particular, it is by such a one speaking about his childhood, so in words of memory, and more particularly, about his first memory of words, say of first acquiring them.*

*Let's have a translation of Augustine's words before us:*

When they (my elders) named some object, and accordingly moved towards something, I saw this and I grasped that the thing was called by the sound they uttered when they meant to point it out. Their intention was shown by their bodily movements, as it were the natural language of all people: the expression of the face, the play of the eyes, the movement of other parts of the body, and the tone of voice which expresses our state of mind in seeking, having, rejecting, or avoiding something. Thus, as I heard words repeatedly used in their proper places in various sentences, I gradually learnt to understand what objects they signified; and after I had trained my mouth to form these signs, I used them to express my own desires.

*The assertions of Augustine's memories are not, rhetorically, accosting, or insisting, as, say, Socrates' interlocutors are in stopping him on the street with their accostive certainties. On the contrary, we need not see at once anything to stop or to puzzle a philosopher, anything he might be finding remarkable about Augustine's words. I note that I had read Augustine's* Confessions *before reading* Philosophical Investigations, *and I remember wondering, philosophically as it were, over his passages concerning time, but not over his passages concerning the acquisition of language. So if there is something disturbing or remarkable about those words, then I am prepared to find that that is itself a remarkable fact about them. As if to suggest: one does not know, in advance, where philosophy might begin, when one's mind may be stopped, to think.*

*Put otherwise: To open this book philosophically is to feel that a mind has paused* here – *which no doubt already suggests a certain kind of mind, or a mind in certain straits. Wittgenstein* has come back *here. Why? If we are stopped to philosophize by* these *words, then what words are immune to philosophical question?*

*Suppose you are not struck by the sheer (unremarkably) remarkable fact that Wittgenstein has set down Augustine's passage to begin with* – *in order, so to speak, to begin by not asserting anything.* I have later come to speak of this theme – sometimes I think of it as the theme of philosophical silence, anyway of philosophical unassertiveness, or powerlessness – by saying that the first virtue of philosophy, or its peculiar virtue, is that of responsiveness, awake when all the others have fallen asleep. *You might in that case find that the book begins with any one of several remarkable things Wittgenstein says about Augustine's passage.*

*He says, for example, that the passage "gives a particular picture of the essence of human language." This doesn't seem obviously true. How does Wittgenstein know this? And if it does give such a picture, what is wrong with that? Is the picture wrong? Is giving a picture a wrong thing to do? Is picturing an essence wrong? Or wrong in picturing language? Or is it the wrong essence?*

*Again, Wittgenstein will speak of Augustine's description as containing a "philosophical concept of meaning" (section 2). Yet Augustine's words seem ordinary enough. They are arch and over-precise maybe, even pedantic. Why does Wittgenstein say "philosophical"?*

*Wittgenstein records other responses he has to Augustine's words, but what interests me already is what Wittgenstein does not say about that passage, having singled it out as philosophically remarkable. He does not say, for example, that it is false, or that there is insufficient evidence for it, or that it contradicts something else Augustine says elsewhere, or that it is unclear, or that it contains an invalid argument. These are familiar terms of criticism in philosophy; and they are strong ones. If any of them does fit a statement, then that statement has been severely and importantly chastised.* This paragraph is specifically dated by its having been taken up, marked especially by its idea of "terms of criticism," as footnote 13 of "The Availability of Wittgenstein's Later Philosophy," first published in 1962, and collected as the second essay of *Must We Mean What We Say?*

*One of Wittgenstein's first responses to Augustine's passage had been to say, "If you describe the learning of language in this way you are, I believe, thinking primarily of nouns like 'table,' 'chair,' 'bread,' and of people's names, and only secondarily of the names of certain actions and properties; and of the remaining kinds of word as something that will take care of itself" (section 1). So one might think that Wittgenstein will criticize the passage as (i.e., that he will use such terms of criticism as) (1) incomplete, though all right as far as it goes, or (2) a faulty generalization. He does not, and it is important that he does not. The avoidance of the obvious here suggests that it is not philosophically clear beforehand what is wrong with Augustine's assertions and that Wittgenstein will not falsify his sense of finding words astray by resorting to an anxiously impatient explanation. To see the intellectual danger, or say emptiness, in imposing a judgment of error (as if the human forms of fallacy, or fallibility, have been well noticed and logged), let's see what is astray in using here either of the expected terms of criticism (i.e., either "incomplete," or "faulty generalization").*

*About (1). Augustine's description, it emerges, is not "all right as far as it goes," even about nouns and proper names. It contains assumptions or pictures about teaching, learning, pointing, naming – say these are modes of establishing a "connection" between language and the world – which prove to be empty, that is, which give us the illusion of providing explanations. Moreover, to the extent that we lack a good idea of what a "complete description" of the learning of a language would be, to that extent we lack a good idea of what we are saying if we criticize a description as "incomplete." Wittgenstein goes on, in section 2, to ask us to "conceive" a set of four spoken words as "a complete primitive language." We will come back to this request, to what it may mean to enter it.*

*About (2). What does "faulty generalization" say? Where does it fit? Take these cases:*

a) *Having drawn five red marbles from a bag of marbles you say, "The marbles in this bag are red."*
b) *"Courses in physics are harder than courses in philosophy."*
c) *"I like European films better than Hollywood films."*

*About a) Suppose the next marble is green. Then it may be said to you: "See. One is green. You're wrong." You might defend yourself by saying: "I thought, could have sworn, that the marbles were all the same color. They were the same in the other bags I opened." That could just be the end of the matter. You accept it as clear that you are wrong, and clear what you are wrong about. And, if you offer an explanation, it is to make clear why you are wrong, even how you could have been wrong about something you were so confident of. Or you might take a different line, and instead of admitting wrong and giving an excuse or explanation, defend your original claim, or something close to it: "Well, one or two might not be red. It's still right to call this a bag of red marbles, and to sell it as such." Again this could be the end of the matter.*

*About b) Suppose someone objects: "Physics 3 is certainly not harder than Philosophy 287." You may reply: "That's not what I mean. Those courses aren't comparable. I had in mind characteristic courses like Physics 106, which is harder than most middle group philosophy courses." Which amounts to saying something like: "Of course, but on the whole they're harder." Here you are accounting for your "wrongness" as a lack of explicitness. Your statement was abbreviated. Perhaps you should have been more explicit. But what you mean was right.*

*About c) Someone objects: "But you hated My Hitler and I know you love Citizen Kane." To which an acceptable (accommodating) defense might be: "True. But I wasn't thinking of such cases; they are exceptions. As a rule I do enjoy European films more."*

*If these are characteristic examples of accusations against generalizations, and of certain excuses or defenses against the accusations, then if Augustine is guilty of faulty generalization, these accusations and defenses should apply to his remarks. Do they? Could Augustine accommodate Wittgenstein's worries by, as it were, saying:*

a´   *[as in the case of the marbles]: "I thought, could have sworn, that all words were uniformly taught."*

or b´   *[as in the case of the courses]: "I didn't mean what I said to apply to each and every word. Words like "to-day," "but," "perhaps," aren't comparable to words like "table," "bread," and so on. On the whole, however, what I said is true."*

or c´   *[as in the case of the movies]: "I wasn't thinking of such words. They are exceptional. As a rule, however, . . ."*

*These defenses don't seem so satisfying now. They do not bring the matter to a close. "Bring to a close" means: With*

*straightforward (empirical) generalizations, the defenses ex-*
*plain how the mistake or the odd case is to be accommodated,*
*explained. But, applied to the case of Augustine's statements,*
*these defenses either make no obvious sense and strike us as false*
*or faked ("I thought all words were taught uniformly" –*
*granted that you had ever given a thought to the matter of how*
*all words are taught, it is hard to imagine that you had ever*
*thought* that*); or they make claims which we wouldn't know*
*how to substantiate ("aren't comparable" –* how *are they not*
*comparable?); or we don't know what weight to attach to them*
(are *the other words "exceptional"?). So: if Augustine is in*
*error, has erred, if something he says has wandered off the*
*mark, is* inappropriate, *we don't know how he can be, can*
*have, what might explain it.*

*This is a more important matter than may at once appear.*
*It suggests that we may at any time – nothing seems special*
*about the matter of false generalization, saying more than*
*you quite know – be speaking without knowing what our*
*words mean, what their meaning anything depends upon,*
*speaking, as it were, in emptiness. For me an intellectual*
*abyss gives a glimpse of itself here, causes an opening before*
*which the philosophical conscience should draw back,*
*stop.*

*Different philosophers have given different lines of explana-*
*tion for falsehood or error or intellectual grief, depending on*
*what they have taken philosophical assertions and errors or*
*griefs to be. For example, Bacon's Idols find the mind variously*
*farced with prejudices and fanaticisms. Locke was less interested*
*in mapping the specific, local, shortcomings of the human*
*intellect than in humbling it, speaking of clearing it of rubbish.*
*Kant seems to have been the first to make the diagnosis of*
*reason's failures an internal feature of tracking reason's powers,*
*developing terms of criticism of intellectual arrogance that*
*show reason to be subject to "dialectical illusion." (Each of*
*these theories of intellectual grief bear comparison with Plato's*
*account of the human subjection to illusion by his construction*
*of the Myth of the Cave.) Wittgenstein is radically Kantian in*

*this regard, but his terms of criticism are, as they must be, specific to his mode of philosophizing.*

Look for a moment at his first response to Augustine's passage, that it gives us "a particular picture" of the essence of human language. We shall return to this term of criticism many times. Here its implication is: What Augustine says (or is remembering about his learning to speak) is not just inappropriate; it is also appropriate, but to something else (something more limited, or more specific) than Augustine realized. In section 3 Wittgenstein puts a response this way: "Augustine, we might say, does describe a system of communication, but not everything we call language is this system." That is not a very clear remark, but it is clear enough to show that it would not even seem to be a comprehensible explanation of the faultiness of a faulty empirical generalization: Suppose for the case of the red marbles we had said: "What you say, in saying the bag is of red marbles, is true of the red marbles in it, for example, true of the five red marbles you have taken from it; but it is not true of the marbles in the bag that are not what we call red; and there are some." This form of explanation, in this context, is, if serious, empty; but if, as likelier, it is parodistic, it rudely implies that what the other has said is empty.

Why is it illuminating, if it is, to say to what it is that Augustine's descriptions are appropriate? Well, obviously, to know the source of appropriateness would be to know how we can have passed it by; how, we might say, its remarkableness, its motivatedness, has been disguised. (This is the role, in other modes of thinking, that a theory of "ideology" is to play. It is a feature of the importance of Freud's discovery of phantasy.) Wittgenstein portrays the disguised remarkableness by noting the presence in Augustine's passage of (1) what Wittgenstein calls a particular way of conceiving language; and, moreover, (2) a way which it is natural or tempting to conceive of it when we are philosophizing about it (writing our Confessions? remembering something? – is it necessary to suppose Augustine is writing about events in his life that he is actually remembering?).

Before going on to comment on each of these points in Wittgenstein's diagnosis, I pause to mark one feature of our progress so far. We began the discussion of the opening of the *Investigations* by asking why Wittgenstein had quoted – brought himself to stop before – certain words of a certain saint. And we were asking how it was that we (he, before the day he stopped) could have passed over those words.

This pair of questions, or rather this double question, has marked my insistence, since the versions of this material in the early 1970s, on the existence of two principal and conflicting ways Wittgenstein shows of taking Augustine's words: either as – as I said earlier – remarkable or as unremarkable. Wittgenstein characteristically says: as philosophical (or metaphysical) or as ordinary. Hume, in the concluding section of Part I of his *Treatise of Human Nature*, speaks of the philosophical (or "refined reasoning") as the "*intense* view of [the] manifold contradictions and imperfections in human reason," and contrasts the intense view with what we may, on his behalf, call the natural or sociable view. These views differ, among other ways, as malady and melancholy differ from cure and merriment. The radical differences between Hume and Wittgenstein on this point are, first, that Hume does not, apparently, find that the philosophical view requires, or allows, a philosophical account; and (or because), second, Hume does not doubt that the intense view is not inferior (intellectually, if not morally) to the natural or sociable view. While both Hume and Wittgenstein see philosophy as an unsociable activity (like most – mostly male? – philosophers; Austin is an exception important to me), Wittgenstein is essentially more distrustful of *this* way of being unsociable. I imagine this is in part a function of the differences between writing half a century before the French Revolution and writing a century and a half after it, when "everyone and no one" as Nietzsche puts it, or "all and sundry" as Emerson had put it, arrogate to themselves the cloak of philosophy – Presidents and Secretaries and Professors of This and That. No wonder professors of philosophy are happier with themselves when they can rely in philosophizing on their technical accomplishments. Part of the discomfort, as well as part of the elation (both are to be distrusted), in reading Wittgenstein is his refusal of, even apparent contempt for, this intellectual reliance, technical or institutional. (This is surely related to Emerson's preaching of Self-Reliance, also part of the discomfort and elation in reading him. Both responses are to be distrusted in his case as well. Both writers, in their relation to, let's say, the systematic, have had good effects and bad. This is, so far, hardly unusual.) It is, I believe, sometimes inferred from philosophy's unsociability that philosophy is inherently, if not quite inveterately, undemocratic. It is a way of putting the motivation of my *Conditions Handsome and Unhandsome* to say that it is meant to make that inference unattractive.

To anticipate further than these notes will reach: Wittgenstein's *Investigations* is designed to show that (what I call) the voices of melancholy and merriment, or of metaphysics and the ordinary (or, as in my "Availability of Wittgenstein's Later Philosophy," the voices of temptation and correctness), are caused by one another, and form an argument that is not to be decided but is to be dismantled. These various characterizations of the voices paired in philosophical argument are not to be dismissed as "merely literary" variations, amounting intellectually or philosophically to the same thing. They are meant to cite the need for an investigation of the voices, even to mark the beginnings of such an investigation.

In my lecture on Kripke's *Wittgenstein on Rules and Private Language* (chapter 2 of my *Conditions Handsome and Unhandsome*), I say of such paired or locked voices that they are engaged in the argument of the ordinary. To bring this juncture of my thinking about up to date (or to 1988), and to indicate where I have (I trust) taken the matter further, and ask that it be taken further still, I quote a pertinent passage from that chapter:

> The altercation over two ways [of taking the Augustine passage] may sound as follows: One observes, "What could be less remarkable than Augustine's remark about his elders moving around and uttering sounds?" Another retorts [intensely, let us now add], "Less remarkable – when we are in a maze of unanswered questions about what *naming* is, what it *is* to call a thing or a person, what constitutes an *object, how* we (with certainty) grasp one idea or image or concept rather than another, what makes a pointer *point*, a talker *mean!*" Nothing is wrong; everything is wrong. It is the philosophical moment. (*Conditions Handsome and Unhandsome*, p. 98)

I will want to come back to this passage.

*Go back to what I presented as Wittgenstein's double way of accounting for the disguised remarkableness in Augustine's passage – that it (1) contains a particular idea of language which (2) seems natural in the act of philosophizing.*

*About (1). "A particular idea of something" is, in Wittgenstein's way of speaking, as much as to say, a particular "picture" of the thing. A point of speaking this way is that it makes me recognize that the idea or picture is* mine, *a responsibility of mine to be responsive to, a piece of my life that is, whether natural or violent, not inevitable, a contingency of having something as constraining (a freighted term of Kant's) as a human life, a life constrained to make itself intelligible (to itself), to find itself in words.* The excited prose of the preceding sentence indicates, I think, the mounting sense of the number of paths leading off from the topics I'm touching upon, here in particular the idea of the human as a life form among others, as described in an essay of mine ("Declining Decline," mentioned earlier) on Wittgenstein as a philosopher of culture. I might say: In noticing distortion in my language I feel thrown back upon myself – except that I am simultaneously thrown forward upon the particular objects I am thinking about, and the particular words in which I found myself thinking about them.

*About (2). Philosophy, on such a view of the process as Wittgenstein's, has no facts of its own. Its medium – along with detecting the emptiness of assertion – lies in demonstrating, or say showing, the obvious. This bears comparison, at some stage, with Heidegger's characterization, scrupulous to the point of the comic, of "phenomenology" early in* Being and Time *(p. 58): "to let that which shows itself be seen from itself in the very way in which it shows itself from itself." Then the question is unavoidable: How can the obvious not be obvious? What is the* hardness *of seeing the obvious? This must bear on what the hardness of philosophizing is – a hardness itself* made *obvious in the* Investigations' *shunning of the technical, one way of stating Wittgenstein's demand upon the ordinary. Whereas other philosophers, on the contrary, find that the technical is indispensable precisely for arriving at the obvious. Is this a conflict about what "obvious" means? (Mathematicians favor the word "obvious." Wittgenstein's rather competing term is "perspicuous." This is an aside for those who are way ahead of us here.) It is, in any case, a philosophical conflict, not to be settled by taking sides. (Thereby hangs another tale, starts another path. For the moment I ask what causes the sensory privileging in the idea of the philosophically hard as "seeing the obvious". When Thoreau is minded to note our philosophical falling off, he sometimes calls us hard of hearing. This fits moments in Wittgenstein at least as accurately as the idea of a difficulty in seeing does. Why don't we say – why do we have no concept of – being hard of seeing?)*

*All this will come back. Let's for now go on to ask how Wittgenstein concretely constructs the picture whose presence in Augustine's passage he finds to account for our passing it by as natural, unremarkable. This task begins explicitly in section 2:*

Let us imagine a language for which the description given by Augustine is right. The language is meant to serve for communication between a builder A and an assistant B. A is building with building-stones: there are blocks, pillars, slabs and beams. B has to pass the stones, and that in the order in which A needs them. For this purpose they use a language consisting of the words "block," "pillar," "slab," "beam." A calls them out; – B brings the stone which he has learnt to bring at such-and-such a call. – Conceive this as a complete primitive language.

Wittenstein will later, in section 48, refer to a related task as "applying the method of section 2." It is the twin of the task he describes as "providing the language game," as called for summarily in section 116: "When philosophers use a word – 'knowledge,' 'being,' 'object,' 'I,' 'proposition,' 'name' – and try to grasp the *essence* of the thing, one must always ask oneself: is the word ever actually used in this way in the language game which is its original home?" Beginning as I have, wishing to make explicit in one or two strokes issues that Wittgenstein allows to develop in steps through scores of examples, this critical example of the builders is not ideal for my purpose of illustrating unobvious obviousness, since it is not obvious that we *can* follow Wittgenstein's order to "Conceive this as a complete primitive language." That will itself prove to be a fruitful uncertainty, but it is at the moment in the way. I will return to it after first interpolating a set of examples that use the "method of section 2," or rather of the twin "providing the language game," and that, in principle, at each use of it arrives at a moment of our acceptance that seems, or soon enough will seem (unless the game is provided ineptly) an instance of the obvious. (In section 48 Wittenstein describes the method as "consider[ing] a language game for which [an] account is really valid.") For this purpose, and again for purposes of locating a region in which to consult further explorations of an issue, I reproduce herewith some stretches of pages 73–5 of *The Claim of Reason*. (It is important to me that the pages concern examples precisely of pointing to something, which is

one of the significant features of Augustine's passage.)
As follows:

> The concept of "pointing to" can be used in conjunction
> with the concepts of such "objects" as colors, meanings,
> . . . places, cities, continents, . . . indeed, it would seem
> you can point to anything you can name. . . . But, of
> course, each of these different "objects" will (= can) be
> pointed to only in definite kinds of contexts. If one thinks
> one or more of these kinds of objects *cannot* be pointed to,
> that is because one has a set idea ("picture") of what
> pointing to something must be (consist in), and that per-
> haps means taking *one* kind of context as inevitable (or one
> kind of object as inevitable) [or one kind of language game
> as inevitable]. For example, if you are walking through
> Times Square with a child and she looks up to you,
> puzzled, and asks "Where is Manhattan?," you may feel
> you ought to be able to *point* to something, and yet at the
> same time feel there is nothing to point to; and so fling out
> your arms and look around vaguely and say "All of this is
> Manhattan," and sense that your answer hasn't been a very
> satisfactory one. Is, then, Manhattan *hard* to point to?
> [What are language games for pointing to a city?]. . . . If
> you were approaching La Guardia Airport on a night flight
> from Boston, then just as the plane banked for its ap-
> proach, you could poke your finger against the window
> and, your interest focused on the dense scattering of lights,
> say "There's Manhattan"; so could you point to Manhat-
> tan on a map. Are such instances not really instances of
> pointing to *Manhattan*? Are they hard to accomplish? Per-
> haps we could say: It feels hard to do (it is, then and there,
> impossible to do) when the *concept* of the thing pointed to
> is in doubt, or unpossessed, or repressed.

Take Wittgenstein's example of "pointing to the color of
an object." In philosophizing one may compare this with
"pointing to the object" and find that it is either difficult to
do (feeling perhaps that a color is a peculiar kind of physical object, a *very* thin and scattered one?) or that it cannot
literally be done at all: to point to the color of an object just
*is* to point to the object (with a special effort of attention

on its color? or saying under your breath "I mean the color"?) [What is the tip-off here that this is in the grip of the *intense* view? I introduced this example with the words "In philosophizing." How do you know when you are philosophizing? For Wittgenstein this is an urgent, definitive question; for others not. Is this a significant difference?] But why? Wittgenstein's explanation is, we know, that "we are misled by grammar," that "we lay down rules, a technique, for a game, and . . . then when we follow the rules, things do not turn out as we had assumed . . . we are therefore as it were entangled in our own rules" (section 125). I wish I were confident that I understood this explanation fully; but what he is getting at is, I think, clearly enough illustrated in the present case. The "rule," the "technique," we have laid down for "pointing to the object," is the trivially simple one of pointing to an object whose identity we have agreed upon or can agree upon with the act of pointing [to that object]. Then we suppose that we follow *this* technique in pointing to that object's color, and when we point to the color according to that rule it seems a *difficult* thing to do (in trying it, I find myself squinting, the upper part of my body tense and still, and I feel as though I wanted to dig my finger into the object, as it were, just under its skin). But one *needn't* become entangled. If we look at the way "Point to the color of your car" is actually used [give its language game; apply the method of section 2; scientists used to call some such things thought experiments; lawyers refer to something of the sort as hypotheticals], we will realize that the context will normally be one in which we do not point to *that* object, but to something else which has that color, and whose color thereby serves as a *sample* of the original. And as soon as we put the request in its normal context [give its language game], we find that nothing could be easier (e.g., the shape of the hand in pointing will be different, more relaxed). And it won't seem so tempting to regard pointing to something, or meaning it, as requiring a particular inner effort – nor to regard a color as a peculiar material object – once we see that, and see how, the difficulty was of our own making. Someone may feel: "Doesn't this show that pointing to a color is, after all, pointing to an object which has that color?" I might reply: It shows that not all cases of "pointing to an object" are cases of "pointing to an object which has a color."

[Does this imply that some objects have no color? And does this mean that some are colorless?] Using the method of section 2, let us imagine a case for which "pointing to an object which has a color" is right. ["Is right" translates "stimmt" in section 2; in section 48 the German for the analogous "is really valid" is "gilt." *Stimmen* and *gelten* are fateful ideas for this fateful point of Wittgenstein's methods, the former invoking voice and conscience and mood, the latter invoking currency and recognition and the worth of questioning – matters broached in *The Claim of Reason* under the rubrics of "the aesthetics of speech," and "the economics of speech,' pp. 94–5.]

. . . The case might be one in which we are shown a group of variously shaped and differently painted blocks and then [when this group is covered or removed] shown a homologous group of unpainted blocks, each of which corresponds in shape to one block in the former group. . . . We are then given a sample color and told "Point to the object which has this color." [I don't say you couldn't poignantly search, as it were, for an absent or invisible (painted) block to point to; in the meantime there is a perfect candidate among the present and visible (unpainted) blocks to point to.] (It may be significant that in the two passages [in the *Investigations*] in which the examples of "pointing to an object" and "pointing to its color" occur, Wittgenstein does not actually provide language games for *pointing* at all, but moves quickly to remarks about *concentrating one's attention*; and at section 33 he goes on to give varying contexts [using the method of section 2] for *that*).

*Now let's go back to Wittgenstein's instruction in section 2 to "Imagine a language for which the description given by Augustine is right." Unlike providing language games for pointing, "imagining a language for which" (and moreover, one which the last sentence of section 2 directs us to "conceive as*

*a complete primitive language") is not something it is clear we
know how to do. Evidently we are to describe a language. Is a
language described in section 2? And, moreover, a complete
one?*

One might say that there is no *standing* language game
for imagining what Wittgenstein asks. Wittgenstein is then
to be understood as *proposing* his game in section 2 as one
which manifests this imagining; it is his invention, one may
say his fiction. That is perhaps the differentiating feature of
"the method of section 2." (Austin, the other candidate I
take as definitive of ordinary language philosophy, does
not go in for such invention. Yet another hanging tale.)
That we can, as speakers, invent language, or let me say,
propose inventions of language, is radically important in
Wittgenstein's "vision of language" (an unguarded phrase
I use in the title of chapter VII of *The Claim of Reason*). But
this is as language-dependent as any other act of speech,
say of speaking ironically, or in tongues. Wittgenstein's
inventiveness may be part of the reason why so many of his
readers get the idea that philosophy, in Wittgenstein's
practice, is a particular language game. I set it down here
as provocation – since it is too early even to begin being
sensible or orderly in exploring the idea – that philosophy,
in Wittgenstein [and in Austin], is the quintessential activity that has no language games of its own; which perhaps
will amount to saying that it has no subject of its own (call
this metaphysics).

This is not to say that in the history of the West philosophy has developed no language of its own, that it has not
proposed concepts of its own. The origin and status of this
language has been the incessant question of philosophy
since, I guess, Plato, until by now it can seem philosophy's
only question. Since it is reasonably apparent that both
Wittgenstein and Heidegger incessantly philosophize by
putting the language of philosophy under fire (from which
it follows that one cannot rest assured that what they are
doing is philosophizing, but that that is an incessant ques-

tion for each of them), and equally apparent that these fires are not the same (both are progeny of Kant's, but not both are progeny of Hegel's), the question is bound to arise (if, that is, one regards these figures as principal voices of the present of philosophy) whether both or neither of the fires will survive when they are turned upon one another. Since I do not believe that the question has yet been fully engaged, I philosophize, to the extent I do, within the sense of a split in the spirit of philosophy, of two live, perhaps dying, traditions that are to an unmeasured extent blank to one another. (And what does literary studies mean by "philosophy"? I do not assume that it means just one thing, nor that it should, nor that it is an "it.")

The endless importance (to me) of thinking within the split mind of philosophy, is something that would be mentioned in the introductory remarks I alluded to at the beginning of these notes. It shouldn't go unsaid. But what then is said? (How does philosophy begin?) I think I understand what it may mean to say that philosophy is a leaking boat that must be repaired while at sea. But what if the edifices of philosophy are in flames, like sections of cities? Shall we hope it is true after all that philosophy begins in water? And what is it that Wittgenstein's builders are building?

*What is described in section 2 seems to be not so much a language as the learning of a language. But then isn't that what Augustine's passage is describing? And Wittgenstein's point in picturing the language for which Augustine's account is right is then to suggest the thought that our idea of what language is is bound up with our ideas of what acquiring language is (and what using language is). (We don't, I believe, say that we* learn *our first language, our mother tongue. We say of a child who cannot talk yet that he or she cannot talk yet, not that he hasn't learned his native language.* If not (quite) as a feat of learning, how do we conceive of our coming into language, or "acquiring" it? I will have a late suggestion about this. *Specifically, the implication is: If language were acquired and used as Augustine's description suggests, then language would be something other than we think it or know it to be – communication, meaning, words, speech, would be different. It would, for example, look like what is going on in section 2.*

*Wittgenstein says of the language there that it is "meant to serve for communication." Evidently he wishes to avoid saying that the builder* is speaking *to his or her assistant. I think one senses why. To "conceive this as a complete language" we have, presumably, to conceive that these people only use their words when they are in* this *situation, doing this work. They cannot then, for example, use the words to "discuss" their work or "reminisce" about past work* – not, at any rate, without inventing (or, as I proposed earlier, proposing) an expression. Perhaps one of them gives the other a look, or nod, in the direction of a certain one or pair of the building-stones, at dawn or dusk, sitting together before or after work. (Wittgenstein is imagining something comparable, I believe, when at section 42 he imagines something he calls "a sort of joke" between the builders; it is a joke, so to speak, about a theory of language as the correspondence of name and thing. As though to suggest: as primitive as having words is having a theory of words and being anxious in the theory.) In speaking of inventing forms of expression, turns of thought, I am, remember, speaking of inventing *currency*, something that *stimmt*s or *gilt*s. Inventing language is not counterfeiting it.

*If this is the way I am to conceive what is happening, then how can I not be in doubt whether these people can speak at all? Those four so-called "words," of which their language is said to consist, then may seem like more or less articulate grunts. Wittgenstein refers to them as* calls *(*Rufe, *as in section 2 and section 6).* Would it be less prejudicial, or less theoretically dangerous, to speak of these things as "signs"; or would it be more prejudicial? We will want eventually to consider Wittgenstein's associating an idea of the sign with an idea of death, as at section 432. How does the association come about? Not, I think, in Wittgenstein, through a philosophical (metaphysical) interpretation of writing. *Are we reluctant to call this a language because its vocabulary is so small? What is our measure here? I feel that the builders' responses (or I picture them so that they) are "too mechanical" for them to be using language, even using* one *word (and is my picture arbitrary?). Does this mean that I am not able to conceive that they* are understanding *their words, and* therefore *not speaking? I can imagine robots, or men hypnotized, doing the things the builders do at the same four calls. What is missing?*

*Wittgenstein at section 5 remarks that "A child uses such primitive forms of language when it learns to talk." And it does seem easy to imagine a child with only four words. (Baby Books list the number of words a child can say. One may ask why keeping such a list stops so soon.) And is there a question about whether the child "understands" the words? I think we do not feel that we have to answer this, because, as Wittgenstein says, the child is "learning to talk" – that is, we do not have to imagine that the child is (yet, exactly) speaking a language, has, as it were, entered the language. The child's language has a future. But when I try to imagine adults having just these words – e.g., the builder and his assistant – I find that I imagine them moving sluggishly, as if dull-witted, or uncomprehending, like cave men.*

*Try it out. Make yourself call out one of your only four words, making one of your only four choices (except for the choice not to work, if that is a choice in those circumstances).* I confess to shuffling slowly down the sides of classrooms moaning out my four "words." *I want this experience in this room to bring itself, in contrast, to the way a child "says" its four words – with what charming curiosity, expectation, excitement, repetitions. . . . The child has a future with its language, the builders have, without luck, or the genius of invention, none – only their repetitions. (We must imagine Sisyphus happy, Camus reports. But isn't that possibility a function of our knowledge that Sisyphus is being punished, hence that he has possibilities* denied *him?* *(The suggestion of the builders as constituting a scene, or allegory, of political denial comes up later, pp. 160–3.)*

*Wittgenstein lets the question of understanding present itself at section 6 – or rather Wittgenstein backs into the question and then backs out right away: "Don't you understand the call 'Slab!' if you act upon it in such-and-such a way?" It is one of Wittgenstein's signature non-rhetorical rhetorical questions designed, among other causes, to elicit conflicting responses within a group, and within an individual, as if to display the farce, and desperateness, of the philosopher's drive to take a side, intensely. Let's give the two conflicting responses.*

*1   One side says: "Acting on the call correctly is understanding the call. What more do you want, or imagine that there is to want?" This seems like something happening in section 1, p. 3, where Wittgenstein says about an implied question of a hearer's understanding: "Well, I assume that he acts as I have described. Explanations come to an end somewhere." This coming to an end (of philosophy, endlessly), is a great theme of* Philosophical Investigations. The theme of ending has struck me as perhaps containing the most telling contrast between this way of philosophizing the overcoming of metaphysics, and other ways, in particular deconstruction's Heideggerean way. I am going to take this up at the end. *But here, in the beginning section of the book, Wittgenstein's remark about coming to an end is comic; no doubt for some it is infuriating. I assume the effect is deliberate. What is the deliberation? This way of taking the question about understanding takes on the familiar reading of Wittgenstein as a behaviorist.* Perhaps this is less common a way of deciding about him than when the lectures represented in these notes were first being given; but it is surely not over. *Wittgenstein allows himself to be questioned about this many times. For example, "Are you not really a behaviorist in disguise?" (section 307). In the present case, however, if he is a behaviorist he is quite without disguise, without clothes altogether. That he can be read without apparent difficulty –*

*sometimes almost irresistibly – as a behaviorist (think of this for now as denying the (independent) reality of our inner lives) is an important fact about his teaching, perhaps something essential to it (as he suggests at section 308). Some of Wittgenstein's followers, as much as some of his enemies, take him so, take him to be asserting (as a thesis, let me say, to mark another path untaken that we must go back to) that "Acting on the order is understanding it." (I assume here that Wittgenstein's (non-)rhetorical question about understanding is not assuming a* definition *of "acting on" which assures that that is not to be taken in a behaviorist way. The untaken path about "theses" is more visibly, if not more clearly, marked at pp. 33–4 of* The Claim of Reason.*)*

2   Other readers, furious at this way of taking or deciding the question, decide the opposite way: "*What* more *do I want? I want* understanding, *something going on upstairs, in the mind!*" Thirty years ago, when this beginning was still beginning for me, I would call such readers "traditional philosophers"; there are vestiges of this habit in the first three parts of *The Claim of Reason.* Traditional philosophy was marked out for me by its blindness or deafness – so I took it – to the modern in letters and in the arts, most particularly to the questioning of the tradition raised precisely in Wittgenstein, and also in Austin. As I came to recognize that I did not know what a tradition is, nor what it takes to overcome tradition, I stopped speaking so, anyway so lightly. What I used to think of as traditional philosophical reading overlaps, I believe, with what today is called "humanism." The mark of this side of things is perhaps expressed – in the present "opposite" (or oppositional) way of making Wittgenstein's question into (or leaving it as) a thesis – by an obsessional searching for mind, innerness, understanding that seems suspiciously close to searching for substance. This search, or temptation, is part of what is under scrutiny in Wittgenstein's interlocutors. "Interlocutor" is the name by which certain quoted voices in the *Investigations* are conventionally

identified by Wittgenstein's readers. Characteristically, I believe, there is in that convention the assumption that there is really one voice, held by an "interlocutor," together with a picture that that figure is someone other than Wittgenstein, which is in a sense true, but in a sense not.

*If I were forced to pick between these alternative decisions – the behaviorist and the anti-behaviorist – I would pick the anti-behaviorist, without a doubt. (The general reason, I think, is that the behaviorist seems to be denying something. Denial generally strikes me as more harmful, more fixated, than enthusiasm.) But not without a qualm.*

*The behaviorist reading gives me a sinking feeling, or a feeling of isolation – as though I am thinking that just possibly it is true that there is no depth to human kind. Wittgenstein can give me this feeling more starkly than behaviorist psychology ever did. I could always dismiss the psychology as mere theory, or what used to be called "methodology." But Wittgenstein carries the suggestion that the option of behaviorism may, as it were,* become *true, that human kind can no longer afford its historical depth, or what it counts to itself as depth.* But can we wait for it to figure itself out here, recount itself? For me this becomes the question whether philosophy is to give way to politics, to give up its patience in favor of the urgency of polemics, of taking sides. As if giving up on the idea that the conditions of philosophy can be achieved through philosophy – which is how I see the "paradox" Plato expressed by the idea of the Philosopher–King. The issue of the intolerability of the price of philosophy, its powerlessness, is the subject of "Emerson's Constitutional Amending."

*The anti-behaviorist reading leaves me cold. What would I get if I decided that way, beyond the idea that understanding isn't* just *behavior, or* merely *or* simply *behavior, or behavior* alone, *or itself? And now instead of there being no depth, or say no soul, the body and the soul are too far apart. The soul is ineffective, a mere hypothesis, which many will conclude that they have no need for, as in the case of God (when God became a hypothesis).*

Let us try to see a little past the edges of the anti-behaviorist fantasy. Let us grant that there is something inside the builders, something we might call "understanding." What might we imagine a candidate for such an object, a meant, a referent, a significate, to be?

A   *Let's suppose it is some mechanism of the brain that establishes a much-needed "connection" between the call and the object it calls for. Of course I know of no such mechanism, nor what any such "connection" might be. It must have* something *to do with the electrical/chemical linkages of nerves; but* some *connection of this kind between calls and objects is patently already in place in the case of the builders; it is what causes my problem with their life. The connection is – what shall I say? – too direct, too hard; it lacks mediation. (Does this equally invite me to imagine something specific going on in the nerves? Something perhaps more devious?)*

*When would saying "There's a mechanism inside" be informative? (What is a language game for this? What is "the role of these words in our language" (section 182).) Take a case: You bring a human-size doll into the room, stand it up, and say to it "Slab!" and "Pillar!" etc., and at each command the doll goes off to the corner of the room and "fetches" back the object named in the call. I am impressed. I ask you how it works and you reply: "There's a mechanism inside." Does this* explain *how it works? It could mean: "You wouldn't understand." It could mean: "It's not a trick" (which might mean that you're not working with a confederate in the basement who holds a magnet under the place the doll is standing and walks the doll, via the magnet, to the correct places). "Try to figure out where a mechanism might be that runs this apparently transparent object" (a toy car, a real clock) is hardly an explanation of its working. In any case, the mechanism of connection is here not* supplying *understanding.*

B   *What else might we feel is missing when we feel that understanding is missing in acting on a call? Wittgenstein's interlocutors sometimes like to introduce the idea of having an image into such perplexities. Would it help in attributing the concept of understanding to the builders if we conceived them to have images of the respective building-blocks on saying or hearing their names? (Wittgenstein raises the question of images so-caused in section 6.)*

*Let's* give *the builder an image, so that instead of, or as supplement to, saying "Slab!" he holds up a painting of a slab. Why not, indeed, supply him with a real slab and with one of each of the other building-stones, and so enable him to hold up an instance of what he wants? This might strike you as better or as worse, from the point of view of establishing communication, or establishing connection. As better: Now a connection is* insured, *he cannot fail to know what I want (that is, can't mistake which one). Or as worse: It makes it seem even harder to establish connection; if there is doubt about the establishing of connection, the doubt deepens or sharpens. Because the doubt is now clearly not whether he knows which one but whether he knows* that I want *the thing I want, and that I want him to respond in such as way as to extinguish my desire. Suppose he stands and admires the picture I present of the object, or else thinks (if I hold up an instance of the object) that I am telling him that I* already have *one, have what I want. How do we imagine that having an image can establish a connection between my words and the desire that my saying them expresses? Might the character of the image enter in? Suppose the builder holds up his instance of the object he wants, e.g., a slab, and exaggeratedly (that is, for the benefit of the assistant) hugs and kisses it. You can see that this is subject to interpretation, and that it might or might not be interpreted to mean that he wants* another *object just like the one he is embracing. Would it help if the image comes up inside the assistant's head? Would greater intimacy of association be established?*

*One is not encouraged, from the fate of these examples, to go on searching for a something – if not a mechanism, or an image, then a meaning, a signified, an interpretant – that explains how calls reach what they call, how the connection is made; searching as it were for a new function for a new pineal gland. The philosophical interest in a philosophical search for a connection between language and mind, and between mind and world, so far as I recognize an intellectual enterprise not taking its bearings from the current institutions of science, is to determine what keeps such a search going (without, as it were, moving). Wittgenstein's answer, as I read it, has something to do with what I understand as skepticism, and what I might call skeptical attempts to defeat skepticism.* Heidegger's answer has something to do with Nietzsche's nihilism, with the metaphysics of the subject, and with the interpretation of thinking as representation. Derrida's answer has something to do with Heidegger's interpretation of Western metaphysics as a metaphysics of presence. I might say that, so far as I have seen, the question "Why does philosophy persist in the search for substances in which understanding, intention, reference, etc. consist?" cannot be satisfied by the answer "Because of the metaphysics of presence." That answer seems to repeat, or reformulate, the question. Say that Wittgenstein shows us that we maintain unsatisfiable pictures of how things must happen. The idea of presence is one of these pictures, no doubt a convincing one. But the question seems to be why we are, who we are that we are, possessed of this picture.

*At some such stage (we must ask what this stage is), Wittgenstein will remind us that there are ordinary circumstances in which (language games in which) we say such things as "B acted as he did (made the connection) because he understood the order, or the hint; he didn't just do it out of luck or entrancement." A case may be of a teacher observing his or her chess student in a difficult game of chess. The student glances at the teacher, the teacher returns the glance and glances away sharply at the student's remaining knight. The student evinces no understanding, looks over the board another instant and smoothly reaches out and makes the move the teacher wanted made. Did the student understand the hint? Didn't he, since he acted on it correctly? But did he act that way* because *he understood? Suppose as he passes the teacher on the way out he says, almost under his breath, "Thanks." Is there any doubt that he understood? Do I wonder whether something was going on, or is, in his mind, upstairs? I suppose not; which is not to say that I suppose that* nothing *was going on, or is. If there is a doubt now, looking inside the student will not reach it.*

We have along the way of these remarks distinguished, among ordinary language procedures, what Wittgenstein calls giving a language game for which an account is right, which resembles what Austin calls "reminding ourselves of what we say when" (something that requires that there be standing, recurrent when's, as in using a present object to point to the color of an absent object), from Wittgensteinian language games that extend to mythological cases (as when we gave the builder's assistant an image in his head, which failed to produce a case of "establishing a connection" amounting to understanding), and both from what I called proposals of scenes which may or may not be satisfying realizations of some form of words (as in the case of the builders taken as illustrating a complete language). It may even now be worth noting that Wittgenstein's idea of a criterion has only with my latest example, that of taking a hint, come well within view, and still quite unthematically or unceremoniously. The example takes the idea that our concept of understanding (our ordinary understanding of understanding) is grammatically related to, or manifested in, the concept of taking a hint, and the scene in question produces a criterion of giving a hint, here a gesture of the eyes in a particular circumstance of obscurity. This production of an instance of our criteria fits Wittgenstein's description of his procedures as producing "reminders," since this chess story could do its work only if we already know what giving and taking hints consist in. We might summarize what we learned from the example in the following form: It is part of the grammar (as described in *The Claim of Reason* at, for example, pp. 70ff.) of following a gesture that *this* is something we call "taking a hint"; which is to say that following the gesture is a criterion of taking or understanding the hint.

We might now find ourselves at the beginning of *The Claim of Reason* – not quite, no doubt, just as it stands – since that beginning rather assumes the importance of criteria for Wittgenstein's understanding of philosophical investigations as matters of grammar. Then this transcription of early lecture notes would have accomplished one of its conscious purposes, to rebegin, or reopen, that material. Unless, however, it turns out that what we have come close to here is, on the contrary, Wittgenstein's understanding of grammar as showing the importance of producing criteria; that is, as showing that what we produce when we consult ourselves (in a certain way) as to what we call something, are precisely criteria, grammatically decisive crossroads. To understand that decisiveness is hardly something for a beginning project, since that issue can be taken as the burden of the whole of Part One of *The Claim of Reason*.

Preparing these pages for the press, in late 1993, I report a new tack begun in a lecture course mostly on the *Investigations* that I offered jointly with Hilary Putnam in the spring of 1993, in which these "Notes and Afterthoughts" were distributed for a week's discussion about halfway through the course. The question whether they actually do represent a reopening of *The Claim of Reason* rather lost its appeal when a representative group of students in the class found the transcription harder to relate to than that book's actual opening. I think I might have found helpful ways to contest that judgment, but in the course of looking for them I came upon the new tack just mentioned. I had not taken it in before that the work of what Wittgenstein calls criteria – for all the importance many of us attach to that development – is (is precisely, I would now like to say) delayed in its entry into the *Investigations*, precisely absent from its opening. Its first appearance, I believe, is at section 51, and it doesn't really get going until some hundred sections later; it may not reach its height until section 580 and following. The significance of this opening or "delayed" absence seems bound up with Wittgenstein's impulse to begin and maintain his thoughts in the region of the "primitive," with a child before the life of language, with workers before their culture's possession (or permitting them possession) of a shared, undoubted language. Imagining, following Wittgenstein's instructions, the primitiveness of the builders – questioning their capacity to understand their words and actions; which is to say, questioning their possession of *words* – is imagining them without the possibility and necessity of exercising judgment, which is a philosophical way of saying: without the possession of (shared) criteria. Their humanity is the stake of the game. Ideas associated with the primitiveness of civilization will take on more life as my transcription proceeds.

My sense of Wittgensteinian criteria, as articulating what in *The Claim of Reason* I come to call our (whose?) agreement or attunement in ordinary words, depends as decisively on appreciating their triviality as much as their importance, their weakness as much as their strength. One could say that their weakness is the source of their methodological strength, small stakes with large shadows. (It may help certain readers of these notes to suggest comparing what "articulating criteria of ordinary words" will prove to mean with what Kant calls providing the "schematism of our concepts.") And since now, a dozen years after the publication of *The Claim of Reason*, and getting somewhat more familiar with the onslaught of French thought over the past quarter of a century, timed in my life from my finishing in the late 1960s the essays in *Must We Mean What We Say?*, I am increasingly aware of a new phase in philosophy's chronic distrust of the ordinary. There is, notably in that strain of radical thought called deconstruction, but widespread beyond that in modern radical sensibilities of other sorts (a point of comparison with certain conversative sensibilities, of whom perhaps Wittgenstein seems one) something I think of as a horror of the common, expressed as a flight from the banal, typically from banal pleasures. It stretches from a horror of the human, to a disgust with bourgeois life, to a certain condescension toward the popular. It is of high importance to me to determine to which of these, or from which, Emerson's aversion to conformity begins. It is with respect to their apparently opposite attitudes toward the ordinary that I have sometimes distinguished the philosophizing of Heidegger and that of Wittgenstein, the former seeking distinction from the ordinary, conceived as "averageness" the latter practicing transformation into it.

But back to my transcription.

*I was saying that we should mark the philosophical "stage" at which we had to remind ourselves of our orientation in the ordinariness of language. I might have described this as remarking our subjection to our language. The stage was one in which the philosophical search for some explanatory substance in the subject (some inner mechanism, image, etc.) came to grief. We might say philosophy had come to a halt, or say that we have had to stop to think. This bears comparison with the stopping or halting we noted as remarkable in Wittgenstein's taking up of Augustine's unremarkable passage. It will help to recognize that Wittgenstein, for all his repudiation of philosophical "theory," intermittently if not continually provides rigorous descriptions of his own practice, which you might call his (or his text's) theory of itself (presumably not of itself alone).*

*Among these self-descriptions of his practice is the following, in a region of the* Investigations *full of such descriptions: "A philosophical problem has the form: 'I don't know my way about'" (section 123). I understand this as a theorization of the search for the beginning of philosophy which produced the beginning of these lectures. It conceives philosophy's beginning for me as one of recognizing that I have lost my way, and in that way am stopped.* This way of putting things is meant, as in *This New Yet Unapproachable America*, pp. 36f., to associate the project or quest of enlightenment, or coming to oneself, in the *Investigations*, fairly immediately with projects portrayed in *The Divine Comedy*, in Emerson's "Experience," and in Nietzsche's *Genealogy of Morals*. *Given this beginning, the end that matches it I take to be given in the preceding section: "The concept of a perspicuous presentation is of fundamental significance for us. It earmarks the form of presentation we give, the way we look at things" (section 122). The progress between beginning and ending is, accordingly, what Wittgenstein means by grammatical investigation, which, since we begin lost, may be thought of as a progress in finding ourselves. (When it comes time to make this less crude, or less abstract, I will be sure not to seem to deny that "perspicuous presentation" might be taken to apply to the whole of Wittgenstein's practice, not solely, even if preeminently, to its (local, momentary – but how does one know that these restrictions contrast with anything?) end.*

Go back to *Wittgenstein's saying that he wants to begin with* primitive *"kinds of application" of words. (The primitive is in principle a far more important theme to work out for the* Investigations *than we have brought out, or will bring out here. It would require accurately characterizing one's sense of the ethnological perspective Wittgenstein characteristically takes toward human kind as such.) He says that beginning with the primitive will "disperse the fog" surrounding the "working of language" produced by "this general notion of the meaning of a word" (section 5) – namely the notion, or the "particular picture of the essence of human language," in which, he goes on to say, "we find the roots of the following idea: Every word has a meaning. This meaning is correlated with the word. It is the object for which the word stands" (section 1). An obvious motive for his description of his motives is to insinuate the idea that there is a "fog" coming in with the general notion of the meaning of a word. And this allows him to sketch a place for the philosophical goal of this motive, namely, to "command a clear view of the aim and functioning of [the] words" (that is, I take it, to arrive at perspicuous presentation).*

*But another motive for stressing the primitive is to prepare the idea of our words as lived, of our language as containing what Wittgenstein will shortly call, in one of his most familiar turns of thought, "forms of life": "To imagine a language means to imagine a form of life" (section 19). As my earlier description of the builders in section 2 was meant to bring out, the clear view we are supposedly initially given is one in which not "merely" the language is primitive, but in which the corresponding life of its speakers is clearly expressed in the language.* We might wish to say that not the language but each word is primitive; the words don't go anywhere. This intuition might come into play when, in discussion, we consider Derrida's idea of the sign as alienated from itself, already elsewhere. This seems to mean something in contrast with Wittgenstein's idea of the primitive.

*Wittgenstein's phrase "form of life" has become a runaway phrase among certain of his readers.* I have since tried to bring a little structure into the discussion of the phrase by distinguishing the ethnological and the biological directions or perspectives encoded in the phrase (in "Declining Decline," pp. 40f.) The ethnological, or horizontal direction (I believe the favored, virtually exclusive, reading) emphasizes differences between cultures, for example, in whether they count or measure or sympathize as we do. The biological, or vertical, direction emphasizes differences between, we might rather say, life forms, for example, as between lower and higher, perhaps expressed in the presence or absence of the hand.

*Let us go back over a way I imagined the lives of the builders in section 2 – as moving laboriously, sluggishly, as if vacantly. This seemed interpretable as their dull-wittedness, as their lacking as a matter of fact (but as a matter of nature, or a matter of history?) a certain power of understanding. I was, it seems, responding to the fact that they only spoke in single "words" or "calls," as if they were incapable of speaking in complete sentences, as if incapacitated or handicapped with respect to a certain kind of performance, of rising to an occasion; as though their words, hence their lives, were forever somehow truncated, stunted, confined, contracted. But there are contexts in which it is perfectly natural for there to be one-word commands or orders. "It is easy to imagine a language consisting only of orders and reports in battle" (section 19). I think of "Forward march," "Enemy at 10 o'clock," "Battle stations." Athletic contests provide another context: "On your marks; get set; go!" There is, I suppose, no reason to think that the builders of section 2 are using "formulas" of this kind.*

*We also know of contexts in which commands or orders are (conventionally?) given in one word where there are no special formulas: e.g., (1) the context, beloved in old movies, of "scalpel," "suture," "wipe"; (2) the context in which builders are doing their jobs in a noisy work area, the context more familiar to us non-primitives, an area surrounded by traffic, spectators, featuring heavy machinery. If in that noisy environment I imagine the calls "Slab," "Pillar," etc., I do not imagine them said sluggishly and vacantly (unless I were to imagine one of the workers ill or drunk), but vigorously, in shouts, perhaps with hands cupped around the mouth. Wittgenstein does not say that his builders are not in such an area. I imagined them alone, and in an otherwise deserted landscape. As though they were building the first building. Was this arbitrary?*

*And why have I not been interested in what they were building, or even that they were building a particular building – for the fact that they are building something in particular would influence the order and repetition and conclusion of the series of "four calls." If I could think of the task as dictating the (order of) the calls, hence of the builder as ready for the next item, I might have imagined him or her differently. Or is it to be supposed that we might merely see (what we perceive as) a "heap" of items mounting at A's location? I gather that I cannot exactly make my perplexity comprehensible to these workers. And can I make myself comprehensible to myself when at the end of the working day the builder and the assistant find a way to climb in carefully among the heap of building-stones and go to sleep? Nor does the heap look like what we think of as a result of* preparing *to build, where stacks of materials are neatly laid. (How do things look at B's location?) For me to imagine their lives, they have to make sense to me. And this seems to me to mean: I have to imagine them making sense to themselves, which is presumably not a gloss I would add were I trying to understand the behavior of bees or beavers.*

*In the cases of the operating room, or the real (noisy) environment, there are obvious reasons why the orders are one-word, or say stylized: to save time, or gain maximum speed and efficiency, to conserve energy. Try it out. Imagine that the workers are on a populous construction site. Now take away the spectators, and traffic, and turn off for the moment the heavy machinery. They may still be doing things essential to the job at hand, but don't we feel that there is no* reason *for them to shorten or stylize their sentences, anyway none beyond the effect of the repetitiveness of the familiar routines themselves? To raise the voice, stylize the sentence, is as inappropriate there, without some practical purpose, as it would be at a concert. That the voice is understood as responsive to its circumstances, but that there is no certainly unambiguous level at which to pitch the voice or fix the distance over which to project it, creates an anxiety expressed in our laugh, familiar at talkies, when one character continues to yell for a few words after a persistent noise suddenly ends, or the distance is closed, that had made the yelling necessary.*

*But it is not accurate, or not enough, to say about Wittgenstein's builders that there is no reason for them to truncate or stylize their sentences. I would like to say that they* just do *speak, or behave, in the way described. But that is our problem. We might express it by saying: They* cannot *behave anyway else, they have no alternative. Earlier we imagined that they do not speak apart from working; now we may imagine that they do not speak differently in noisy than in peaceful environments. They are not* free. *Maybe this is the sense of their behaving "mechanically" that I expressed earlier;*

*and maybe this lack of alternative is the way to describe what* *was missing for me when I agreed that I missed a sense of* *understanding in them. But what is the connection between* *understanding and having or seeing an alternative? There is a* *connection between interpretation and seeing an alternative,* *since interpretation is a matter of taking something one way* *rather than another. Perhaps the connection with the case of* *understanding is that the alternative to carrying out an order is* refusing *to carry it out, disobedience to it. Disobedience has* *been taken (in Eden, to divine command; in Kant's moral* *philosophy, to inclination) as a criterion of freedom. But which* *comes first? Earlier I felt that without endowing the builders* *with understanding I was not fully prepared to say that they* *were speaking, and hence not prepared to see them as fully* *human. But now what emerges is that I did not see them as* *human because they did not seem to me to have freedom.* And now I feel I want to go beyond the thought that freedom is shown in the capacity to say no, to the thought that it is shown in saying no in one's own voice (responsive to different circumstances, capable of distinguishing consent from duress) – perhaps related to the cause of Emerson's and Nietzsche's search for a ground on which to say yes, the yes they took as the sign of a human existence, that thinkers before them, whom they were going beyond, not repudiating, had taken as the sign of a political existence.

In somewhat intensifying the linking of understanding with freedom, and in the explicit emergence of the connection of having a voice and with having a political existence (a connection stressed, but not systematically pursued, early in *The Claim of Reason*, pp. 22–8), I am prompted to interpolate here parts of a long paragraph from the Wittgenstein lecture in *This New Yet Unapproachable America*; the passage (pp. 62–4) is the most recent in which I have put into print thoughts about the builders:

One may well sometimes feel that it is not language at all under description [in the Augustine passage] since the words of the language . . . seem not to convey understanding, not to be *words*. . . . But while this feeling is surely conveyed by the scene, . . . we need not take it as final, or unchallenged, for at least three lines of reason: (1) [There follows a lightning rehearsal of the figures of the primitive or "early human," of the sense of truncation in the calls in different environments, of the child with four words, ending:] Instead of the feeling that the builders lack understanding, I find I feel that they lack imagination, or rather lack freedom, or perhaps that they are on the threshold of these together. (2) Something *is* understood by the builders, that desire is expressed, *that* this object is called for. . . . Therewith an essential of speech is present, a condition of it, and not something that can, as new words are taught, be taught. ("Therewith"? There I am taking the builders also as illustrating Augustine's scene as of an advent of language (challenging a picture of the accumulative "learning" of language), something that comes "with" an advent of the realm of desire, say of fantasy, "beyond" the realm of (biological) need. I have been instructed, here particularly concerning Freud's concept of *Trieb*, spanning the "relation" between biological and psychological drive, by the exceptional study of Freudian concepts in Jean Laplanche's *Life and Death in Psychoanalysis*.)

[The instruction I speak of, as it enters, for example, into the scare quotes I have set in the previous sentences around "with" and "relation," etc., calls particular attention to Augustine's description of the use to which he puts the names he has lined up with the objects his elders line them up with, the description that ends the Augustine passage: "After I had trained my mouth to form these signs, I used them to express my own desires." The part of the picture of language here, forming other "roots" of the idea or philosophical concept of meaning Wittgenstein divines in Augustine (and evidently not there alone), is something like this: The preparation for my acquiring language is my possession of a structure of desires and a nameable world; when I have acquired my set of signs, I may then use them to insert those desires into that world. Then again I may not. What determines whether I invest in the world, say yes to my existence? When (historically) did this become an issue? (My little book on Thoreau's writing, *The Senses of Walden*, is, perhaps above all, about this investment, something I call (roughly in Thoreau's name) taking an interest in the world; this is not so much a cure of skepticism as it is a sign of its mortality. In *In Quest of the Ordinary*, I comparably take up in this relation to skepticism Wordsworth's declaration of his wish "to make the incidents of common life interesting" (pp. 6–7). The figure of the child, under the shadow of such questions, returns yet again at the end of these notes.)]. . . . (3) A further, non-competing interpretation of the builders is as an allegory of the ways many people, in more developed surroundings, in fact speak, forced as it were by circumstances to speak in more or less primitive, unvaried expressions of more or less incompletely educated desires – here the generalized equipment of noise and the routines of generalized others, are perhaps no longer specifiable in simple descriptions, having become invisible through internalization. (Is it theory that is wanted, more than fuller description?) [If there is a theory it must, I suppose, be understandable as one that demonstrates the modes whereby, in Foucault's words, power "reaches into the very grain of individuals, touches their bodies and inserts itself into their actions and attitudes, their discourses, learning processes and everyday lives."] This allegory may be seen as a kind of political parody of the repetition (or say the grammar) without which there is no language. (I take the workers as political allegory in terms that allude to Heidegger's description of the everyday ("generalized equipment," "noise") in order to indicate a possible site of meeting, or passing, of Wittgenstein and Heidegger on the topos of the everyday – a place from which it can be seen both why Heidegger finds authenticity to demand departure and why Wittgenstein finds sense or sanity to demand return.)]

*From a certain point of view, especially in certain moods of philosophizing, it would hardly occur to us to think that radical conceptual differences – for example, between calling something a language or not, or between calling a creature human or not – could turn on whether these creatures speak differently (for example, use different tones of voice) in noisy and in quiet environments. It would seem that when we "took away" the familiar, or everyday, or "natural" context in which the builders would speak in single words, we were taking away only something inessential, trivial, quite external – the builders are surely the same, surely they are* doing *the same thing, their* behavior *is the same, whatever their tone of voice? And yet the lack we felt in trying to attribute understanding to the builders, which we sought to compensate for by imagining some inner mechanism or image, was filled up precisely, i.e., it quite vanished, as we (re)supplied "outer" surroundings.*

*The mutual regulation of inner and outer is a great theme of the* Philosophical Investigations, *specifically forming the background against which criteria function – against which they do the little, the indispensable little, they do to keep body and soul, or world and mind, together.* Since a version of this theme motivates the opening – the direct discussion of criteria – of *The Claim of Reason*, we are again at a goal of this transcription of these lecture notes. That discussion of criteria in *The Claim of Reason* reaches a plateau at the conclusion of chapter 4; it starts up afresh, in the form of an extended discussion of privacy, as the beginning of Part Four.

*The sense of the builder's lack of freedom is confirmed, as suggested earlier, by Wittgenstein's description (in section 6) of this language as the* whole *language of a tribe. He says there that "the children are brought up to perform* these *actions, to use* these *words as they do so, and to react in* this *way to the words of others." Surely it is easy to feel here: This group would have to exert great efforts to suppress certain natural responses of the children.* It suggests itself that a perception housed in this feeling gives on to an idea that the concept of the natural at some point becomes linked (dialectically or not) with the concept of transgression. Suppose this link is expressed in the Kantian picture of discovering the limits of knowledge, to transgress which is to enter one of several systematically related forms of madness (dialectical illusions). (As if it is nature itself (herself?) which has become the thing-in-itself.) And suppose we give a sexualized reading (roughly what Laplanche calls a perverse reading, in his interpretation of Freud's mapping of the human creation of, i.e., the creation of human, "drives") of the violence exercized in the course (or curriculum) of "being brought up to perform, use, react" in prefigured ways certain actions, words, and reactions. Then we perhaps have a way, in what I sometimes speak of as "our" part of the forest, of coming to see what Foucault means (and he seems to be speaking out of a thriving culture in his part of the forest – what is the conviction that these are parts of the same expanse of thought?) in speaking of Sade's placement, in the discovery of sexuality, of "that firmanent of indefinite unreality . . . , the discovery of those systematic forms of prohibition which we now know imprison it, the discovery of the universal nature of transgression." (I've been reading Foucault's "Preface to Transgression," in *language, counter-memory, practice*, ed. Bouchard.)

*So that the training of children is a process of stupefying them into the state in which we encounter the grown-up builders. I do not, in these fantasies, wish to appear extreme. We need not imagine the grown-ups, the representative men and women (presumably there are women) of the builder's culture, taking brutal measures in moulding their charges. If the charges are recalcitrant, that is to say, fail the test of serious participation in performing, speaking, reacting, as the elders require, the consequences may be merely that the elders will not speak to them, or pay them full attention, or else that they perpetually express disappointment in the children, and tell them they are bad. As our kind mostly does.*

## II

With that last paragraph (whose rhetoric I recognize as going with the sketches of children in the ending paragraphs of Part One, chapter 5 of *The Claim of Reason*, hence as dating from 1970–1, when that material was being revised into its present form), I come to the end of the notes I had chosen to transcribe. The notes for the lectures that continue from there take up various specific topics of the *Investigations*, versions of many of which found their way into the early chapters of *The Claim of Reason*, others of which became the general sketch of Wittgenstein's "vision of language" that forms chapter 7, and still others constitute the opening couple of dozen pages of Part Four. What follows here may be thought of as an epilogue to the transcription, unless indeed it is better thought of as an introduction to the interventions that intersperse the transcription, interventions without which I would not have been able to provide it, i.e., to deliver the lectures from where I now find myself.

The 1984 instance of my Wittgenstein lectures was the last time they were given. It was also, as said at the beginning of these notes, the first time they were given after the publication of *The Claim of Reason* and where the foregoing reported material was explicitly cast, often confusedly, as I recall the occasions, as an attempt at a new, or alternative, beginning to my text. It was the first time, as well, that I began to indicate how I might relate the problematic of skepticism in my view of Wittgenstein to the view in Kripke's *Wittgenstein on Rules and Private Language* (published in 1982 – I had heard a lecture of Kripke's on the subject in 1976). The first published account of that relation constitutes chapter 2 of *Conditions Handsome and Unhandsome*. Given the existence of the books of mine just listed, I had thought to let the present occasion come to an end here.

But one line of thought, or emphasis, that I began, or first made explicit in an extended form, in 1984, has become increasingly critical for me, and I want to end with some speculations that get it into more attention, if not into better focus. It concerns the remarkable fact of the presence of the figure of the child in Wittgenstein's thoughts, announced with its opening quotation from Augustine. It is not a figure one expects to find in philosophical texts; I suppose the causes of its absence, so to speak, will differ in the divided traditions of philosophy, ones not very helpfully named the Continental and the Anglo-American traditions. Its absence in the latter, say in what is called, also not very helpfully, analytical philosophy, is something that prevents that mode of philosophy from recognizing psychoanalysis as one of its others. In my own case, my interest in ordinary language philosophy has from the beginning been tied up with the idea of the child as a necessary figure, however obscure and untheorized, for philosophy's stake (or repression of the stake) in the ordinary.

A comparatively early epitome of this preoccupation of mine sounds this way at the end of Part One of *The Claim of Reason*:

> The examples of "knowing how to continue" give a simple or magnified view of teaching and learning, of the transmission of language and hence of culture. It is a view in which the idea of *normality*, upon which the strength of criteria depends, is seen to be an idea of *naturalness*. It isolates or dramatizes the inevitable moment of teaching and learning, and hence of communication, in which my power comes to an end in the face of the other's separateness from me.
>
> Wittgenstein's idea of naturalness is illustrated in his interpretation of taking a thing to be *selbstverständlich*: "The rule can only seem to me to produce all its consequences in advance if I draw them as a *matter of course*" (section 238). I know the series, I can continue with a

word, when, for me, the continuity is a matter of course, a *foregone* conclusion. In the series of words we call sentences, the words I will need meet me half way. They speak for me. I give them control over me. . . . That is what happens to my power over the pupil; I give it over to the things I am trying to convey; if I could not, it would not be that thing. . . .

Children's intellectual reactions are easy to find ways to dismiss; anxiety over their "errors" can be covered by the natural charms of childhood and by our accepting as a right answer the answer the child learns we want to hear . . . By the time the charm fades, their education takes place out of our sight.

When my reasons come to an end and I am thrown back upon myself, upon my nature as it has so far shown itself, I can, supposing I cannot shift the ground of discussion, either put the pupil out of my sight – as though his intellectual reactions are disgusting to me – or I can use the occasion to go over the ground I had hitherto thought foregone. If the topic is that of continuing a series, it may be learning enough to find that I *just do*; to rest upon myself as my foundation. But if the child, little or big, asks me: Why do we eat animals? or Why are some people poor and others rich? or What is God? or Why do I have to go to school? or Do you love black people as much as white people? or Who owns the land? or Why is there anything at all?, I may feel run out of reasons without being willing to say "This is what I do" (what I say, what I sense, what I know), and honor that. (p. 122, pp. 124–5)

The sub-text of such thoughts is the section of the *Investigations*, cited earlier, that runs: "If I have exhausted the justifications I have reached bedrock, and my spade is turned. Then I am inclined to say: 'This is simply what I do' " (section 217). In my chapter on Kripke's Wittgenstein, (*Conditions Handsome and Unhandsome*, chapter 2) where I in effect begin my opposition to his interpretation by re-reading this passage, I call the passage Wittgenstein's scene of instruction. The details of my opposed sense are not to the point here. But that chapter ends with another phase, begun in *This New Yet Unapproachable America*, of my interest in Wittgenstein's interest in the Augustine passage. I quote two excerpts from the closing paragraphs:

The stake for me in [Wittgenstein's] scene of instruction is that it specifies Augustine's description of his learning of language, the opening words of *Philosophical Investigations*, as that of a scene of instruction, a scene that haunts the *Investigations* as a whole, since Augustine's words precisely announce the topics of the book as a whole. I recite Augustine's (translated) words: when, my, elders, name, some, object, accordingly, move, toward, something, I, saw, this, grasped, called, sound, uttered, meant, point, intention, shown, bodily movements, natural language of all peoples, expression, face, eyes, voice, state of mind, seeking, having, rejecting, words, repeated, use, proper places, various sentences, learnt, understood, signified, trained, signs, express my own desires. . . . (*Conditions Handsome*, p. 98)

This time around, for some reason, what strikes me about Augustine's description is how isolated the child appears, training its own mouth to form signs (something you might expect of a figure in a Beckett play), the unobserved observer of the culture. The scene portrays language as an inheritance but also as one that has, as it were, to be stolen, anyway in which the capacity and perhaps the motivation to take it is altogether greater than the capacity and perhaps the motivation to give it. Haunting the entire *Investigations*, the opening scene and its figure of the child signals that the question "Where did you learn – what is the home of – a concept?" may at any time arise (and not only in the couple of dozen sections in which the child explicitly appears), that the inheritance of a culture – the process of cultivation (or what is the point of spading?) – comes not to a natural end, or rather to its own end, but to one ended, by poor resources, or by power; that when explanations in particular circumstances run out, teaching becomes heightened while control over what it is that is taught, say shown, is lessened. (*Conditions Handsome*, p. 98, p. 99)

And this time around there is something else, a hint of permanence in the child's isolation, the absoluteness in its initial incapacity to make itself known, in its absolute reliance on its elders' recognition of its attempts at expression, that is, on their recognition of the grip of its needs as the medium of expression, that leads me to understand the child as mad, not exactly deranged, but in the condition of derangement.

In the background of this perception is the experience of Melanie Klein's accounts of the pre-verbal child's development of experience in terms of paranoia and depression, and of Laplanche's description of the "perversion" of instincts into drives in the infant's turning to the human. The idea of derangement, containing the idea of undoing (or, in Emerson's image, circumscribing) a circle or ring, can accordingly mark the turn to the human and its speech as renouncing the unending circle of the animal, the realm of the untalking subjects, of the repetitive cycles of need and satisfaction, or their end. Kant speaks of this trauma of the advent of the human as "reason [doing] violence to the voice of nature . . . to the . . . subjection to instinct" ("Conjectural Beginning of Human History," trans. Fackenheim, in L. W. Beck ed., *Kant on History*, p. 56). Kant speaks of this violence, as befits his moral theory, as something human adults, with their claims of reason full-blown, ask of themselves. Now we can allow ourselves to see it as what is asked of the human in infancy, as if prematurely, as everything about the human is premature.

Something of this idea was there the last time (in my chapter on Kripke) I reported my encounter with Wittgenstein's adoption, I mean adapting, of Augustine's childhood, as if recognizing that both childhood and madness together haunt the *Investigations*, that the so-called interlocutor's voice can sometimes be heard as the voice of madness, and sometimes as the voice of childhood. ("What if one insisted on saying that there must also be something boiling in the picture of the pot?" (section 297).) The presence of the idea shows, I think, if all but unnoticeably, in the second paragraph of the excerpt I just quoted from myself, in the phrase "to be stolen," associated with the idea of inheritance.

I have since writing that paragraph composed two texts that bear on that association, and completing them has prompted my first reading, as usual awkwardly late, if not premature, of two well-known papers, one by Derrida on Artaud, one by Foucault on Laplanche's study of Hölderlin, which seem to me, in turn, to bear interestingly on the way I have lately been reading the child at the beginning of the *Investigations*. One of the texts of mine ("In The Meantime," written for the Whitney Humanities Center at Yale, in February of 1991, published the following year in *The Yale Journal of Criticism*) ends by taking up exlicitly our most famous site of the association of theft and inheritance and language, the story of Rebecca's arranging that Jacob rather than Esau receive Isaac's blessing. I ask there whether we are really to believe that, since Isaac says, "The voice is Jacob's voice, but the hands are the hands of Esau," blind Isaac really believes that the one before him is Esau, that is, really to believe that Isaac trusts the hand more than the voice?

The other of my texts about theft and voice and something like tradition (specifically, it concerns what Emerson calls "The Spirit of the Age"), is the reading of Emerson's "Fate" in which I take up Emerson's implicit linking of words, hence the possibility of thinking, with a certain form of breathing ("Emerson's Constitutional Amending," cited earlier, p. 16). The form of breathing (of spirit) is one that opposes the breath in my body – in my words, say my voice – to the ideas that fill the common air, as if the individual voice and the cosmic air are essentially equal antagonists. Emerson discerns the air as "full of men," a reading of it as announcing his (so America's) belatedness, hence as naming the ideas taken into his lungs and voice, which he calls receiving impressions, as plagiarized. But it remains in doubt who steals, whether it is I who deplete the common stock, or whether the common air, being fully spoken for, a plenum, prevents any from being mine, so suffocates me.

Reading Derrida's paper on Artaud is what sent me back to my description of Augustine's child – if it is to talk – as in the position of stealing language. Derrida calls his text "La parole soufflée," and it works, as may be imagined, through the complexities of the word *soufflée*, most particularly, and most impressive to me, its invitation to be translated as "spirited away." An essential path Derrida takes from this is to Artaud's madness as an interpretation of the age as stealing his breath, perhaps because it poisons the air, perhaps because it cannot live with his. In my perception of Wittgenstein's/Augustine's child, the sense of one's language as stolen is the ground of our doubt that any thought is really ours, as though everything I know is telepathic, and that to be known is to have my mind read. Then I am horribly vulnerable to other minds. It would be well if they did not exist.

Derrida's text refers to Foucault's "The Father's 'No'," on Laplanche's study of Hölderlin's madness. (That I told myself I had not read the Derrida because I hadn't sufficiently studied Artaud; and not read the Foucault because I hadn't a good enough chance to understand Hölderlin; are familiar forms of banality among the reasons philosophers give themselves for their ignorance; there are also excellent reasons. I tell of the banalities here because of their bearing on the question where philosophy begins, since it cannot read the *first* word. But why I let Derrida be the last straw in the present case should be accounted for; this is for another time.) Given the persistence – perhaps it will prove to be a creative intensification – of the rift in the culture of Western philosophy, I must expect that someone who knows Foucault, and so on, way better than I may nevertheless profit from these pages of mine. In that case it is not vain to include here some initial reactions to certain of Foucault's formulations, taking for the moment the following passages:

> More than simply an event that affected our emotions, that gave rise to the fear of nothingness, the death of God profoundly influenced our language; the silence that replaced its source remains unpenetrable to all but the most trivial works. . . . Hölderlin's language replaced the epic unity commemorated by Vasari with a division that is responsible for every work in our culture, a division that links it [Hölderlin's language?] to its own absence and to its dissolution in the madness that had accompanied it from the beginning. ("The Father's 'No'," in *language, counter-memory, practice*, p. 86)

> As a Christianized Europe first began to name its artists, . . . Vasari's *Vite* sets as its goal the evocation of an immemorial past. . . . Genius makes itself known from infancy, not in the psychological form of precocity, but by virtue of its intrinsic right to exist prior to its manifestation in specific accomplishments. Genius is not born, but appears without intermediary or duration in the rift of history; similar to the hero, the artist sunders time so as to reestablish its continuity with his own hands. . . . The heroic dimension passed from the hero to the one whose task it had been to represent him at a time when Western culture itself became a world of representations. A work no longer achieved its sole meaning as a monument, a memory; it now belonged to the legend it had once commemorated. . . . [The painter's] self-portrait was no longer merely a marginal sign of the artist's furtive participation in the scene being represented . . . ; it became . . . the totality of the painting where the beginning joins the ending in the absolute heroic transformation of the creator of heroes.

> In this fashion, the artist was able to develop a relationship to himself within his work that the hero could never experience. (ibid., pp. 72–4)

If the language of philosophy is one in which the philosopher's torments are tirelessly repeated and his subjectivity is discarded, then not only is wisdom meaningless as the philosopher's form of composition and reward, but in the expiration of philosophical language a possibility inevitably arises: . . . the possibility of the mad philosopher.

But what language can arise from such an absence? And above all, who is the philosopher who will now begin to speak?

The eye in Bataille delineates the zone shared by language and death, the place where language discovers its being in the crossing of its limits . . . the turning back of language upon itself at the moment that it fails – . . . the association . . . of sight to truth. . . ." ("Preface to Transgression," in *language, counter-memory*, p. 44, p. 41, p. 48, p. 49)

These thoughts, so far as I have so far grasped them, apply more directly to the treatment of skepticism within *The Claim of Reason* as it stands – where madness is associated, reading Wittgenstein's *Investigations*, with ideas of limits, hence of transgression, with language turning upon itself, with a craving for emptiness or for escape from the human which is interpretable as a craving for the death of the human, and with the temptation to speak outside language games – than they do to the alternative beginning to *The Claim of Reason* represented by these notes. Yet those thoughts of Foucault seem to me to support my sense of the child as the opening figure, even hero, of the *Investigations* as essentially subject to the philosophical madness which ensues.

In response to the idea of genius making itself known from infancy by virtue of its intrinsic right to exist prior to its manifestation in specific accomplishments, I think both of Augustine's isolated child divining words of others, and of Emerson's idea of genius as the capacity, in principle universal among human kind, for the individual to believe that claiming his or her own language, speaking for oneself, is the same as the power to speak for others, in principle universally – a capacity requiring genius now precisely because nothing assures or grounds it, which is the predicament Kant discovered as the condition of speaking (as in aesthetic judgment, and moral judgment) with the "universal voice." Since the Augustine passage is about an infant who will become an elder who speaks for philosophy, and is autobiographical, it must form part of an undertaking to show how he acquired the authority to speak philosophically, for example to speak philosophically of this acquisition; and in taking his childhood as exemplary in its acquiring the right to speak, he is claiming that the philosophical subject is the human subject itself. These are features of Augustine's discourse pertinent to the topics and the procedures of Wittgenstein's *Investigations*, a discourse in which Wittgenstein sees "a particular picture of the essence of human language [in which] we find the roots of the following idea" (something about the meaning of a word being the object it stands for). This remarkable finding on Wittgenstein's part, or this invention of a remarkable discourse in which to express his finding, precisely avoids saying that Augustine has presented a theory of language, advanced or primitive, but implies, since the roots holding it in place seem so unobjectionable, that they are ones apt to be found in or beneath any such theory. It seems to me, indeed, to be the theory of language, call it language as reference, or truth as adequation, that so much of post-structuralist thought is designed to oppose. (For example, it seems that Wittgenstein's idea of the enforced metaphysical consequences of attempting to speak outside language games is some specification of Derrida's attack on what he calls the transcendental signified. But just what relation "some specification of" names is nothing if not an open question.) I have offered the thought that the words of the Augustine passage announce the words of the major part (Part One) of the *Investigations*. It follows from that thought that the uncovering of the idea whose roots are in those words is not accomplished prior to the work of that entire part.

Foucault's conjunction of the death of God, the absence of philosophically grounded language, and the figure of the mad philosopher, whose language turns upon itself, as if to exhaust itself, suggests to my mind a further pressure on Wittgenstein's choice of the beginning passage from Augustine, one bearing precisely on something not said in that paragraph but something said in a previous paragraph in the same section of Augustine's *Confessions* from which the one Wittgenstein cites is taken. It is also a passage about the teaching of language, hence also about language as such. (Put less archly, as earlier, though for those not familiar with Wittgenstein perhaps less communicatively, "hence about language as such" means, in Wittgenstein's lingo, that the concept of teaching language is grammatically related to the concept of language.) The previous passage from Augustine's *Confessions* goes as follows (I repunctuate, and add phrases in brackets, to bring out my understanding of what is being said):

> . . . my elders did not teach me words in any set method, as they did letters afterwards; but I myself, when I was unable to say all I wished and to whomsoever I desired (by means of the whimperings and broken utterances and various motions of my limbs, which I used to enforce my wishes), repeated the sounds [which were] in my memory by [virtue of] the mind, O my God, which thou gavest me.

(I note, for future reference, the clause "did not teach me words in any set method." The comparison with teaching "letters," which I assume means teaching the reciting of the alphabet, suggests that "set method" means, or includes, "correct order." I shall not try here to determine whether Augustine is suggesting that there is some such order of words and that his elders were neglectful in not finding or not imposing it, or whether he is noting that of

course, come to think of it, there is no correct order of
words, e.g., no first and no last, as there are in the order of
letters. This question arises in my chapter on Kripke's view
of Wittgenstein on rules and privacy, cited earlier, in its
noting a difference, within a similarity, between an arith-
metical function and a concept of ordinary language.)

The obvious difference between this passage from Augustine and the passage Wittgenstein begins with lies in
this one's appeal to God, both passages addressing the
distance between a desire, or order, and the object or the
person in mind (the distance between, as I put it with
respect to the builders, signified and significate). Recall
Foucault's sense that "the death of God profoundly influenced our language; the silence that replaced its source
remains unpenetrable . . .". I take Wittgenstein's quoting
of his Augustine passage, after the death of God (hence
after it became impossibile to quote, to similar effect,
Augustine's previous passage), to bring the questions it
contains into the ensuing (modern) realm of silence, of
sourcelessness. There is nothing whereof one cannot
speak; therefore one must attain silence.

A few moments ago I raised the issue of Augustine's
autobiography as raising for him the question of his authority in speaking (specifically in speaking of his acquiring language) philosophically. I am for myself convinced
that Wittgenstein, in incorporating Augustine's words as
his initiating topics, incorporates as well (or finds that he
has incorporated, in the work making up *Philosophical
Investigations*) the autobiographical as essential to the work
of philosophy, or say recognizes the fate of philosophy to
be linked with the necessity of confession. Ordinary language philosophy systematizes, abstractly, this use of the
so-called first person. The method of language games, or
the kin (Austinian) method of saying what we should say
when, are nothing, not even one man's opinion, let alone
the sublime acts of arrogation they turn out to be, unless
they are games that I imagine myself to play, words I find

I have it in mind, or at heart, to say. (This sense of
philosophy as autobiography and arrogation is the opening
topic of my "In the Meantime," cited earlier.)

It is common, even pleasant, to say that Wittgenstein
writes well, even with genius. It is something else to try to
specify the pressures under which his writing is made. I
shall specify three such pressures, giving expression, let's
say, to three forces, all but incessantly entangled. I have
called them (most lately in "Postscript (1989): To Whom
It May Concern," *Critical Inquiry*, Winter 1990) first, the
voice of temptation; second, the voice of correctness; and
third, the attainment of silence, say unassertiveness, a
heightened rhetorical field which does not present itself as
a voice). It may help us see the significance of writing that
is thus responsive – or help us see that Wittgenstein's
invention of it is not a contingent fact about his thinking –
if we recall Foucault's linking of the artist's taking over of
the heroic dimension to the advent of the self-portrait "no
longer [as] a marginal sign of the artist's furtive participation in the scene being represented [but as] the totality of
the painting" [now become the site of a heroic transforma-
tion]; and recall that Foucault identifies this site as that of
madness and of what becomes of the possibilities of philosophy. This makes possible for Foucault his formulation
of "the language of philosophy [as] one in which the
philosopher's torments are tirelessly repeated and his subjectivity is discarded," a formulation which Foucault apparently found his way to in thinking about Bataille, but
which seems unusually apposite to a quality of depth in
Wittgenstein's writing that could hardly be more plain and
hardly more resistant to a clear account.

It is out of such a sense of undefined depth in
Wittgenstein's writing, and of his condition, or fate, of
artistry, that I was led, for example, the last time I encountered the passage in which the writer of the *Investigations*
expresses the exhaustion of justification with the image of

his spade being turned, to identify his spade as a figure for his pen. (*Conditions Handsome and Unhandsome*, p. 79)

Before pressing that identification a step further here, I should perhaps take a question I imagine coming my way: "If you, for whatever reason, arrive at such identifications from within a sense of Wittgenstein's text as it has been received, and filtered, within Anglo-American institutions of philosophy, why seek the ratification, or company, of opposed, Continental institutions? Can this be worth the awkwardness of citing works that others have known, and know the provenance of, longer and better than you? Why glory in your belatedness, a poor thing?" I suppose the answer depends on what one takes philosophical work to be. Since I have said that the rift within the philosophic mind, expressed as one between shunning traditions, seems to me a philosophical reality, a reality of Western philosophizing now, to go on with philosophy presents itself to me as a function of going on within the experience of this rift – which for me does not mean looking for more translations from one bank to the other, unless a translation could give incomprehension palpability (thinking of F. Schlegel's dislike, I think one might even say horror, of what is called comprehension). To live within this rift, to the meager extent open to me, means, for example, precisely to entertain such a question of worth as I just took on. It is a question sometimes of entertaining bad voices, not just, as in the case of Wittgenstein's interlocutors, voices expressive of false need, whose direction it is up to you to contest, but voices of false promise, whose future is unresponsive to your desire.

Among the other untaken paths I wish to imply, my invoking of "Western" philosophy just now is not something I would like to be seen as (though in part it cannot help but be) an allusion to the Heideggerean–deconstructive critique of "Western metaphysics." It is directly, however distantly, a result of my continuing experience with the writing of Emerson and of Thoreau which continuously makes itself aware of Eastern philosophy, more familiar a gesture in nineteenth-century than in twentieth-century philosophy (surely not just for discreditable reasons). This awareness prompted my linking, in *The Senses of Walden*, structural and philosophical features of *Walden* with the *Bhagavad-Gita*; and caused, in the Epilogue to *Conditions Handsome and Unhandsome*, a reading of one of Emerson's counter-Christian, here Persian, parables – one it happens, about the madness and justice in philosophizing. I am taken back to my sense of one of Wittgenstein's reflexive descriptions of his thinking ("What we are destroying is nothing but structures of air [Luftgebäude]") as harboring something I call, in the Introduction to *The Claim of Reason*, a "Zen sound." My sense is based on the following Zen story, whose provenance I cannot attest to, and which I heard no later than in my graduate school days. Not uncharacteristically of me, especially at certain periods of my life, I did not tell the story at the time I based a thought upon it, because I imagined that everyone knew it; that is, that I was the last to hear. This is the story. The Master said: "A goose is in a bottle. How do you get it out? Quick! Quick!" The pupils present were unable to speak. The Master responded: "Open your mouth and let it out." The interpretation of the story ran along reasonably predictable lines. The goose's predicament is produced by words; let the words go. I am sure a part of me still imagines that a knowledge of this story helped Wittgenstein to his image of showing the fly the way out of the fly-bottle.

We have, about at the end, come upon the subject of the culture of philosophy, call it the conditions or the curriculum of philosophy, the subject of what a philosopher is to know, given the unlikelihood, even for Heidegger or for Wittgenstein, of succeeding in knowing and reading, respectively, everything or nothing. Allow me to go over, a little less reticently, an identification I proposed in a passage from *Conditions Handsome and Unhandsome* that I cited a while ago (p. 169): "Haunting the entire *Investigations*, the opening scene and its figure of the child signals that the question 'Where did you learn – what is the home of – a concept?' may at any time arise . . . , that the inheritance of a culture – the process of cultivation (or what is the point of spading?) – comes not to . . . its own end, but. . . ." In what sense is the identification of spading with cultivation really in the *Investigations*, in the lines "If I have exhausted the justifications I have reached bedrock, and my spade is turned. Then I am inclined to say: 'This is simply what I do' "?

But even apart, for the moment, from the (allegorical) identification of the spade with the philosopher's pen, what causes the inclination to express my exhaustion of justifications by a demonstrative in the direction of what I do? What do I do that I imagine might yet attract your interest? And what is my interest that I am willing to have patience, to suffer, apparently indefinitely, until you find yours? If something was interesting when my digging was producing justifications, is something interesting about the fact that I have stopped? If my spade is a philosophical instrument, then presumably it was digging in the light of providing edification, or say nourishment. And how did my justifications become exhausted? Who spoke first, the philosopher or the neighbor; the author of *Philosophical Investigations* or the author's interlocutor; the child or the teacher; Wittgenstein or Augustine; sanity or madness? Have I intervened in the child's life with a judgment (probably of disapproval, but approval might equally have been impertinent)? Or has the child asked a question (or made an assertion, which might come to the same)? I am asking what *attracts* the child to my plot. Why does he or she care what I know, or think, or do, that I should be inclined to rest upon it, in his or her view? If what I do is interesting, is it something like fixing a bicycle, or like comforting an animal? Is it perhaps impressive, like wearing a uniform or wielding a sword; is it fascinating, like swallowing the sword? Is it thrilling, like a pillow fight, or a cartoon of a bear rising to fall on an intruder; is it amazing, like a man imitating a machine, or vice versa; is it a cause of wonder, like a man sitting still in some attactive spot in the woods?

How do we represent one another, become "representative men"? How, for example, do I come to "stand for humanity," as Emerson puts it, where this means not just being a sign of the human (as if it does not yet exist), nor simply of a culture that forks men and women one way rather than another; but of an originality to be forgone – traumatically but perhaps ecstatically – in sharing the breath of a culture? How is my becoming lost within a culture represented by my being unfound by language, as if the originality expressed in madness is the image of the breath I require if I am not to suffocate in the conformity exacted by culture? It is the measure of my distance from myself, my splitting, my guilt, as of the theft of my language, my right to speak, to exist, that makes possible, and necessitates, my letting you represent my possibility, the fact that I (too) am a sign – let you return to me my rejected thoughts with an alienated majesty, constrain me to another standard than I have come to understand. (This "return" and "constraint" are allusions to passages of Emerson I have interpreted elsewhere, for example, in "Emerson's Aversive Thinking," chapter 1 of *Conditions Handsome*.)

Our representativeness of one another has presented itself to philosophers, from Plato to Kant, and from Hegel and Marx and Kierkegaard to Emerson and Thoreau, and in a sense to Nietzsche and Heidegger and Wittgenstein, as projecting another world, or another dispensation of culture. This is the culture that moral perfectionists inevitably call for, the culture that is not appalled by our mad origins, that is revolted, yet sane, in the face of culture's current dispensation (artistic and political) and that promises us expression, breath.

Is Wittgenstein's interest in the nativity of our native language naive? What is it – for one who supposes so – that Wittgenstein fails to know? That ordinary language is controlled by forces it does not know? That some of these forces are metaphysical? Ordinary language philosophy makes certain intelligent people as nervous as deconstruction does. Each view seems open to annihilation by some well-placed one-line death-blow (perhaps to the same, perhaps to a different selection of these people). I have witnessed a prominent, self-named decontructionist write on a blackboard a list of such one-liners against deconstruction (e.g., "Deconstruction thinks language is meaningless"; "Deconstruction thinks one text is as good as another"; "Deconstruction thinks one interpretation is as good as another"; etc.) and then demolish each in turn with textual evidence and heavy mockery; whereupon, in turning to Austin on speech acts, and noticing his appeal to ordinary langauge, this teacher asked, lightly mockingly, "Whose ordinary language?" – as if the question of the right to speak for others had never crossed Austin's mind.

I have been coming across musicologists who take the trouble to deny that *Meistersinger* is more naive than *Tristan*. Evidently someone has been affirming that it is more naive, as though a recurrence to the diatonic was retrograde once thorough-going chromatic procedure had been established. What was this affirmation assuming? That Wagner failed to know this, that perhaps he had forgotten it?

You can see that I am having trouble ending, even a text so readily nameable as the transcription of some early lecture notes on a well-known philosophical text. Sensing this process of transcription as one of delivering the lectures, my pedagogical impulse, matching the wish to show as well as to point out and to theorize the question of philosophy's beginning, is to show as well as to point out and theorize the question of philosophy's consequent ending.

I said that the theme of the coming to an end of philosophy contained perhaps the most telling contrast between the traditions of philosophizing represented by Heidegger and by late Wittgenstein (from the period of the *Investigations* on). A recent moment at which I was led to try to locate this contrast occurs near the end of "Declining Decline," as follows:

> What Wittgenstein means by speaking outside language games, which is to say, repudiating our shared criteria, is a kind of interpretation of, or a homologous form of, what Spengler means in picturing the decline of culture as a process of externalization. . . . In the *Investigations* Wittgenstein *diurnalizes* Spengler's vision of the destiny toward exhausted forms, toward nomadism, toward the loss of culture, or say of home, or say community. He depicts our everyday encounters with philosophy, say with our ideals, as brushes with skepticism, wherein the ancient task of philosophy, to awaken us, or say bring us to our senses, takes the form of returning us to the everyday, the ordinary, every day, diurnally. Since we are not returning to anything we have known, the task is really one, as seen before, of turning. The issue then is to say why the task presents itself as returning – which should show us why it presents itself as directed to the ordinary. (pp. 65–6)

[Wittgenstein] is joining the fate of philosophy as such with that of the philosophy or criticism of culture, thus displacing both – endlessly forgoing, rebuking, parodying philosophy's claim to a privileged perspective on its culture, call it the perspective of reason (perhaps shared with science); anyway forgoing for philosophy any claim to perspective that goes beyond its perspective on itself. This is its poverty of perspective. But what makes this poverty philosophy?

I say that this philosophy lies in its practice, the commitment to go on in a certain way, call this discontinuously, which is to say, not in an endless deferring of a claim that might as well be a gesture toward infinity, say transcendence; it lies rather in a particular refusal of endlessness, in an unguardedness, an openness. (A gesture toward an endlessness of deferral, an infinite, so toward some transcendent, seems to occur in the writing of Derrida; but then that work exactly questions an older philosophical gesture of transcendence. I have to think about this remembering Austin's exasperation voiced more than once, about philosophers who insist that there are infinite uses of language – doubtless he would have had in mind Wittgenstein's saying, early in the *Investigations* (section 23) that there are "countless" kinds of use – or that the "context" of a use is infinitely complex, as a way to defer getting down to the business of counting them. My love for Austin's gesture here did not stop me from asking myself – wasn't I supposed to? – what philosophy's business then is.) It is the practice that constitutes diurnalization, a way or weave of life to challenge the way or weave that exhausts the form of life of talkers. This is how I understand Wittgenstein's claim to give philosophy peace (section 133). It is not that philosophy ought to be brought as such to an end, but that in each case of its being called for, it brings itself to an end. (pp. 73–4)

The difficulty of ending is, I guess, the hardest of philosophy's difficulties to bear. Kierkegaard famously rebuked the Hegelians for their endless promises that the system would complete itself. Struck by the paradoxicality of Wittgenstein's tormented claim to bring philosophy peace, a philosopher might find the obligation to end, unsystematically, as one of suggesting endless ends. (This is a motive for the repeated gesture of motioning toward untaken intellectual paths. Not that the gesture need be false; there are such paths. The question is why anyone would suppose that others fail to know that paths are lines of choice, or fate.) But is that really more difficult, or intellectually richer, than acknowledging the end at hand, this moment of ending, without – so far as you know – reserve; that is, without knowing that there will be a time for further words? Falling silent so, letting the others air their words, may well strike one as giving up the ghost.

Differences between the prose of Wittgenstein and that of, say, Derrida, may be attributed to (putting on its polite face) a difference in their concepts of time. The less polite face of the difference shows writing as a function of the address to death – terms in which to give it admission, in which to understand, perhaps to underwrite, the conditions of finitude; terms in which, on which, in the realm of the talkers, silence is best set aside.

# Stanley Cavell: *A Bibliography* 1958–1994

*Compiled by Peter S. Fosl and Michael Payne*

## 1958

1 'Must We Mean What We Say?' *Inquiry* 1.3 (Autumn), 172–212. Reprinted in *Ordinary Language*. Ed. Vere Claiborne Chappell (Englewood Cliffs, NJ: Prentice-Hall, 1964), 75–112; in *Must We Mean What We Say?* (1969), 172–212; and in *Philosophy and Linguistics*. Ed. Colin Lyas (London: Macmillan, and New York: St Martin's Press, 1971), 166–89. Translated as 'Mussen wir meinen, was wir sagen?', in *Linguistik und Philosophie*. Eds Günther Grewendorf and Georg Meggle.' (Frankfurt: Athenaüm Verlag, 1974), 168–219.

## 1962

2 'The Availability of Wittgenstein's Later Philosophy'. *The Philosophical Review* 71 (January), 67–93. Reprinted in *Wittgenstein: The Philosophical Investigations*. Ed. George Pitcher (Garden City, NY: Doubleday, 1966), 151–85; and in *Must We Mean What We Say?* (1969), 44–72. Translated as 'Der Zugang zu Wittgensteins Spätphilosophie'. In *Über Ludwig Wittgenstein*. Ed. Ulrich Steinworth (Frankfurt am Main: Suhrkamp Verlag. 1968), 119–53.

**1964**

3   'Existentialism and Analytical Philosophy'. *Daedalus* 93.3 (Summer), 946–74. Reprinted in *Themes Out of School* (1984), 195–234.

**1965**

4   'Austin at Criticism'. *The Philosophical Review* 74.2 (April), 204–19. Reprinted in *Must We Mean What We Say?* (1969), 97–114; in *The Linguistic Turn*. Ed. Richard Rorty (Chicago: University of Chicago Press, 1967 and 1992), 250–60; in *Philosophy Today No. 1*. Ed. Jerry H. Gill (New York: Macmillan, 1968), 81–101; and in *Symposium on J. L. Austin*. Ed. K. T. Fann (London: Routledge and Kegan Paul, 1969), 59–75.

5   'Aesthetic Problems of Modern Philosophy'. In *Philosophy in America*. Ed. Max Black (Ithaca, NY: Cornell University Press), 74–67. Reprinted in *Must We Mean What We Say?* (1969), 73–96.

**1967**

6   'Music Discomposed'. In *Art, Mind, and Religion*. Eds W. H. Capitan and D. D. Merrill. (Pittsburgh: University of Pittsburgh Press), 69–97. Reprinted in *Must We Mean What We Say?* (1969), 180–212.

**1969**

7   *Must We Mean What We Say? A Book of Essays*. (New York: Charles Scribner's Sons). Reprinted 1976 (Cambridge: Cambridge University Press).

**1971**

8   *The World Viewed: Reflections on the Ontology of Film*. (New York: The Viking Press). Reprinted 1974, 1977,

1979. Selections reprinted as 'Sights and Sounds' in *Aesthetics: A Critical Anthology*. Eds George Dickie and Richard J. Sclafani (New York: St Martin's Press, 1977, 1989), 366–83; and in *Film Theory and Criticism: Introductory Readings*. Eds Gerald Mast and Marshall Cohen. (Oxford: Oxford University Press [1974], second edition, 1979) 306–20.

## 1972

9    *The Senses of* Walden. (New York: The Viking Press). Reprinted 1974 and in an expanded edition 1992.

## 1974

10    'More of *The World Viewed*'. *Georgia Review* 28:4 (Winter), 571–631. Reprinted in expanded edition of *The World Viewed* (1979).

## 1976

11    'Leopards in Connecticut'. *The Georgia Review* 30 (Summer), 233–62. Revised and reprinted in *Pursuits of Happiness* (1981), 111–32.

## 1978

12    'What Becomes of Things on Film?' *Philosophy and Literature* 2.2 (Fall), 249–57. Reprinted in *Themes Out of School* (1984), 173–83.

## 1979

13    *The Claim of Reason: Wittgenstein, Skepticism, Morality, and Tragedy*. (Oxford: The Clarendon Press). Reprinted 1982.

14    'Epistemology and Tragedy: A Reading of *Othello*'

(with a Cover Letter to Molière's *Alceste*). *Daedalus* 108.3 (Summer), 27–43. *Othello* material reprinted from Part IV of *The Claim of Reason* (1979) and reprinted in *Disowning Knowledge* (1987), 125–42. Cover Letter reprinted in *Themes Out of School* (1984).

15    'Thinking of Emerson'. *New Literary History* 11.1 (Autumn), 167–76. Trans. as 'Reflexions sur Emerson et Heidegger', *Critique: Revue générale des publications française et étranger* 36.399–400 (Juin–Juillet, 1980), 719–29. Reprinted in *The Senses of Walden* (1972).

16    'On Makavejev on Bergman'. *Critical Inquiry* 6.2 (Winter), 305–30. Reprinted in *Themes Out of School* (1984).

17    'Pursuits of Happiness: A Reading of *The Lady Eve*'. *New Literary History* 10.3 (Spring), 581–601. Revised and reprinted in *Pursuits of Happiness* (1981), 45–70.

18    'Die Welt durch die Kamera gesehen'. Portions of 'More of *The World Viewed*' (see 10), trans. Lore Iser. In *Theorien der Kunst*. Eds Dieter Kenrich and Wolfgang Iser (Frankfurt am Main: Suhrkamp Verlag, 1979), 447–90.

## 1980

19    'A Reply to John Hollander'. *Critical Inquiry* 6.4 (Summer), 589–91. Reprinted in *Themes Out of School* (1984), 141–4.

20    'Knowledge as Transgression: Mostly a Reading of *It Happened One Night*'. *Daedalus* 109.2 (Spring), 147–75. Revised and reprinted in *Pursuits of Happiness* (1987).

## 1981

21    *Pursuits of Happiness: The Hollywood Comedy of Remarriage*. (Cambridge, MA: Harvard University Press).

Trans. Christian Fournier and Sandra Laugier as *A la Recherche du Bonheur* (Paris: Cahiers du Cinema, 1993).

22    'Foreword' to Jay Cantor, *The Space Between: Literature and Politics* (Baltimore: Johns Hopkins University Press), ix–xv. Reprinted in *Themes Out of School* (1984).

23    'North by Northwest'. *Critical Inquiry* 7.4 (Summer), 761–76. Reprinted in *Themes Out of School* (1984), 152–72, and in *A Hitchcock Reader*. Eds Marshall Deutelbaum and Leland A. Poague. (Ames: Iowa State University Press), 249–64.

### 1982

24    'Genteel Responses to Kant? In Emerson's "Fate" and in Coleridge's *Biographia Literaria*'. *Raritan* 3.2 (Fall), 34–61. Reprinted in *In Quest of the Ordinary* (1988), 27–49; and as 'Emerson, Coleridge, Kant' in *Post-Analytic Philosophy*. Eds John Rajchman and Cornel West. (New York: Columbia University Press, 1985), 84–107. Trans. Oliver R. Scholz and Eckhard Lobsien in *Romantik Literatur und Philosophie*. Ed. Volker Bohn. (Frankfurt am Main: Suhrkamp Verlag, 1987), 183–212.

25    'The Fact of Television'. *Daedalus* 111.4 (Fall), 75–96. Reprinted in *Themes Out of School* (1984), 235–68.

26    'Politics as Opposed to What?'. *Criticial Inquiry* 9.1 (September), 157–78. Reprinted in *The Politics of Interpretation*. Ed. W. J. T. Mitchell (Chicago: University of Chicago Press, 1983), 181–202; and in *Themes Out of School* (1984), 27–59.

### 1983

27    ' "Who does the wolf love?" Reading *Coriolanus*'. *Representations* 3 (Summer), 1–20. Reprinted in

*Themes Out of School* (1984), 60–96; in *Disowning Knowledge* (1987), 143–78; and in *Shakespeare and the Question of Theory*. Eds Patricia Parker and Geoffrey Hartman. (New York: Methuen, 1987), 245–72.

28    'The Thought of Movies'. *Yale Review* 72.2 (Winter), 181–200. Reprinted in *Themes Out of School* (1984), 3–26.

## 1984

29    *Themes Out of School: Effects and Causes*. (San Francisco: North Point Press). Reprinted 1988 (Chicago: University of Chicago Press).

## 1985

30    'What Photography Calls Thinking'. *Raritan* 4.4 (Spring), 1–21. Reprinted in *Raritan Reading*. Ed. Richard Poirier (New Brunswick, NJ: Rutgers University Press, 1990), 47–65. Trans. Klaus Feichtenberger as 'Denken – was heißt das in der Fotografie'. In *Camera Austria* (Graz, Österreich: Forum Stadpark, 1986), 32–43.

31    'A Reply to Robert Mankin on *The Claim of Reason*'. *Salmagundi* 67 (Summer), 90–6.

32    'Being Odd, Getting Even'. *Salmagundi* 67 (Summer), 97–128. Trans. Herbert Hrachovec as 'Danebenstehen, gleichziehen: Bedrohungen der Individualität'. In *Wo steht die Analytische Philosophie heute?* Eds Ludwig Nagl and R. Heinrich. (Wein/München: Oldenborg).

33    'A Capra Moment'. *Humanities* 6.4 (August), 3–7.

34    'Philosophy's Two Myths of Reading'. *The Agni Review* 22, 139–41.

35    'The Division of Talent'. *Critical Inquiry* 11.4 (June), 519–38.

**1986**

36    'In Quest of the Ordinary: Texts of Recovery'. In
      *Romanticism and Contemporary Criticism*. Eds Morris
      Eaves and Michael Fischer. (Ithaca, NY: Cornell
      University Press), 183–239.

37    'The Fantastic of Philosophy'. *The American Poetry
      Review* 15.3 (May–June), 45–7. Reprinted in *In
      Quest of the Ordinary* (1988), 181–8.

38    'Hope Against Hope'. *The American Poetry Review*
      15.1 (January–February), 9–13. Reprinted in *Con-
      ditions Handsome and Unhandsome* (1990), 129–
      38.

39    'Being Odd, Getting Even (Descartes, Emerson,
      Poe)', revised version of 32. In *Reconstructing Indi-
      vidualism: Autonomy, Individuality and the Self in West-
      ern Thought*. Eds Thomas C. Heller, Morton Sosna,
      and David E. Wellbery (Stanford: Stanford University
      Press), 278–313. Reprinted in *In Quest of the Ordi-
      nary* (1988), 105–49.

40    'Hamlet's Burden of Proof'. *Hebrew University Studies
      in Literature and the Arts* 14 (Fall), 1–17. Reprinted in
      *Disowning Knowledge* (1987), 179–91, including a
      'Postscript', 189–91.

41    'Observations on Art and Science'. *Daedalus* 115.3
      (Summer), 171–7. Reprinted in *Art and Science*. Ed.
      Stephen Richard Graubard (Lanham, MD: Univer-
      sity Press of America), 171–7.

42    'Questions and Answers'. In *Romanticism and Con-
      temporary Criticism*. Eds Morris Eaves and Michael
      Fischer (Ithaca, NY: Cornell University Press), 225–
      39.

**1987**

43    *Disowning Knowledge: In Six Plays of Shakespeare.*
      (Cambridge: Cambridge University Press). Trans.

Jean-Pierre Maquerlot as *Le Déni de Savoir* (Paris: Editions du Seuil, 1993).

44   *Nach der Philosophie: Essays von Stanley Cavell.* Eds Kurt Rudolf Fischer and Ludwig Nagl. (Wein: Verlag des Verbandes der wissenschaftlichen Gesellschaften Österreichs).

45   'Notes after Austin'. *Yale Review* 76.3 (Spring), 313–22.

46   'Psychoanalysis and Cinema: The Melodrama of the Unknown Woman'. In *Images in Our Souls: Cavell, Psychoanalysis and Cinema.* Eds Joseph H. Smith and William Kerrigan. (Baltimore: Johns Hopkins University Press), 11–43.

47   'Freud and Philosophy, a Fragment'. *Critical Inquiry* 13.2 (Winter), 386–93.

48   'How can one inherit Europe? Stanley Cavell über Tradition und Neubeginn der amerikanischen Philosophie' [an interview with Leonhard Schmeiser]. In *Nach der Philosophie: Essays von Stanley Cavell.* Eds. Kurt Rudolf Fischer and Ludwig Nagl. (Wien: Verlag des Verbandes der wissenschaftlichen Gesellschaften Österreichs), 219–28.

## 1988

49   *In Quest of the Ordinary: Lines of Skepticism and Romanticism.* (Chicago: University of Chicago Press).

50   'The Uncanniness of the Ordinary'. *The Tanner Lectures on Human Values VIII.* Ed. Sterling M. McMurrin. (Salt Lake City: University of Utah Press/ Cambridge: Cambridge University Press). Reprinted in *In Quest of the Ordinary* (1988), 153–78.

51   'Psychoanalysis and Cinema: "The Melodrama of the Unknown Woman" '. In *Die Philosophen und Freud. Ein offene Debatte.* Eds H. Vetter and Ludwig Nagl. (Wien/München: Oldenborg). Expanded version in

*The Trial(s) of Psychoanalysis*. Ed. Françoise Meltzer. (Chicago: University of Chicago Press), 227–58.

52  'Two Cheers for Romance'. In *Passionate Attachments: Thinking about Love*. Eds Willard Gaylin and Ethel Persons. (New York: Free Press), 85–100.

53  'Declining Decline: Wittgenstein as a Philosopher of Culture'. *Inquiry: An Interdisciplinary Journal of Philosophy and the Social Sciences* (Norway) 31.3 (Spring), 253–64. Expanded and reprinted in *This New Yet Unapproachable America* (1989).

54  'The Advent of Video'. *Artspace* 13.2 (May–June), 67–9.

55  'Conference on Religion and Education' [A discussion with Daniel Callahan, Denise Carmondy, Michael Fishbane, Stephen Richard Gaubard, James Gustafson, Timothy Healy (SJ), Robert Kiely, George Lindbeck, Robert Lynn, Frank Manuel, John Padberg (SJ), and Theodore Sizer]. *Daedalus* 117.2 (Spring), 1–146.

## 1989

56  *This New Yet Unapproachable America: Lectures after Emerson after Wittgenstein*. (Albuquerque, NM: Living Batch Press, and Chicago: University of Chicago Press). Trans. Sandra Laugier-Rabaté as *Une nouvelle Amérique encore inapproachable* (Combas: Editions de l'Eclat, 1991).

57  'Who Disappoints Whom?' On Allen Bloom's *The Closing of the American Mind*. *Critical Inquiry* 15.3 (Spring), 606–10.

58  'Naughty Orators: Negation of Voice in *Gaslight*'. In *Languages of the Unsayable: The Play of Negativity in Literature and Literary Theory*. Eds Sanford Budick and Wolfgang Iser. (New York: Columbia University Press), 340–77.

59  'An Interview with Stanley Cavell' (with James

Conant). In *The Senses of Stanley Cavell*. Eds Richard
Fleming and Michael Payne. *Bucknell Review* 32.1
(Lewisburg, PA: Bucknell University Press), 21–72.

60    'A Conversation with Stanley Cavell on Philosophy
and Literature' (with Michael Payne and Richard
Fleming). In *The Senses of Stanley Cavell*. Eds
Richard Fleming and Michael Payne. *Bucknell Review*
32.1 (Lewisburg, PA: Bucknell University Press),
311–21.

## 1990

61    *Conditions Handsome and Unhandsome: The Constitu-
tion of Emersonian Perfectionism*. (Chicago: University
of Chicago Press). [The Paul Carus Lectures, 1988.]
Reprinted 1991 (Peru, IL: Open Court). Trans.
Christian Fournier and Sandra Laugier as *Conditions
Nobles et Ignobles*. (Paris: Editions de l'éclat, 1993).

62    'Ugly Duckling, Funny Butterfly: Bette Davis and
*Now, Voyager*'. *Critical Inquiry* 16.2 (Winter), 213–
47.

63    'Postscript (1989): To Whom It May Concern'. *Critical Inquiry* 16.2 (Winter), 248–89.

64    'Letter to the Editors: Reply to Tania Modleski'.
*Critical Inquiry* 17.1 (Fall), 238–44.

## 1991

65    'Emerson's Aversive Thinking'. In *Romantic Revolu-
tions*. Ed. Kenneth R. Johnstone *et al.* (Indiana University Press), 219–49. Revised and reprinted as
'Aversive Thinking: Emersonian Representations in
Heidegger and Nietzsche'. In *Conditions Handsome
and Unhandsome* (1990), and *New Literary History*
22.1 (Winter, 1991), 129–60.

66    'The Idea of Home'. *Social Research: An International
Quarterly of the Social Sciences* 58.1 (Spring), 9–10.

67 'Stella's Taste', on *Stella Dallas*. In *Working Papers in Cultural Studies* 8. The Cultural Studies Project. (Cambridge, MA: MIT Press).

## 1992

68 *Status d'Emerson: constitution, philosophie, politique.* Trans. Christian Fournier and Sandra Laugier. (Combas: Edition de l'Eclat). [Includes a translation of 'Emerson's Constitutional Amending'.]
69 'In the Meantime: Authority, Tradition, and the Future of the Disciplines'. *The Yale Journal of Criticism* 5.2 (Spring), 229–37.
70 'L'Humeur Emerson'. *Critique: Revue générale des publications française et étranger* 48 (Juin–Juillet), 541–2. [Trans. Sandra Laugier and Christiane Chauviré of 'An Emerson Mood' from *The Senses of* Walden. *An Expanded Edition*, 1992.]
71 'Macbeth Appalled (I)'. *Raritan* 12.2 (Fall), 1–15.

## 1993

72 'Macbeth Appalled (II)'. *Raritan* 12.3 (Winter), 1–15.
73 'Stanley Cavell' [interview]. In Giovanna Barradori, *The American Philosopher*. (Chicago: University of Chicago Press), 118–36.

## 1994

74 *A Pitch of Philosophy.* (Cambridge, MA: Harvard University Press). [The Jerusalem–Harvard Lectures].
75 'Nothing Goes Without Saying', reading the Marx Brothers. *London Review of Books* 16.1 (6 January), 3–5.

# Index